Department of Health and Welsh Office

CODE OF PRACTICE
Mental Health Act 1983

Published March 1999, pursuant to Section 118 of the Act

London: The Stationery Office

© Crown Copyright 1999

Published for the Department of Health and Welsh Office under licence from the Controller of Her Majesty's Stationery Office

Applications for reproduction should be made in writing to The Copyright Unit, Her Majesty's Stationery Office, St Clements House, 2-16 Colegate, Norwich, NR3 1BQ

Sixth impression 1999

ISBN 0 11 322111 8

FOREWORD

People with mental health problems deserve good care and support.
They are often vulnerable, may have difficulty in expressing their
needs and, in some cases, may not recognise that they need help. These
patients, carers, and the general public, should be able to rely on
health and social services which provide effective care and treatment.

At the moment, the legal framework that managers, doctors, nurses,
social workers and the police must follow is set by the Mental Health
Act 1983. The Code of Practice gives guidance on how the Act should
be applied. It should be used by everyone who works with people with
mental health problems, whether or not they are patients formally
detained under the Act. The Act is increasingly out of date and we are
consulting extensively before changing the law to replace it with a
more modern and dependable system, but in the meantime, the Code
should be followed until the new legislation comes into force.

This revised Code updates and amends the previous version to take
account of recent case law and changes in practice and terminology
since it was last revised in 1993.

For patients and their carers what matters is their own experience of
services and the way that the law is applied in their case. This revised
Code puts a new emphasis on the patient as an individual – from the
guiding principles in the first chapter, through assessment for
admission, consent to treatment, discharge and after-care. It is also
essential that the different agencies that deal with people with mental
health problems work together.

The Code provides essential reference guidance for those who apply the
Act. Patients and their carers are entitled to expect professionals to
use it.

Frank Dobson   Alun Michael

Contents

LEAVING HOSPITAL

PARTICULAR GROUPS OF PATIENTS

Mental Health Act 1983 Code of Practice

INTRODUCTION

Introduction

1.   This revised Code of Practice has been prepared in accordance with section 118 of the Mental Health Act 1983 by the Secretary of State for Health and the Secretary of State for Wales, after consulting such bodies as appeared to them to be concerned, and laid before Parliament. The Code will come into force on 1 April 1999. The Act does not impose a legal duty to comply with the Code but as it is a statutory document, failure to follow it could be referred to in evidence in legal proceedings.

2.   The Code provides guidance to registered medical practitioners, managers and staff of hospitals and mental nursing homes and approved social workers (ASWs) (who have defined responsibilities under the provisions of the Act), on how they should proceed when undertaking duties under the Act. It should also be considered by others working in health and social services (including the independent and voluntary sectors), and by the police.

3.   The Code makes a number of references to the Memorandum on Parts I to VI, VIII and X of the Act (revised 1998) which gives a detailed description of some of the Act's provisions. Authorities, Trusts and other service providers are responsible for seeking their own legal advice on any matters of doubt.

4.   The Secretaries of State are required to keep the operation of the Code under review. The Mental Health Act Commission will be monitoring experience of using the Code and will take this into account in drawing up proposals for any necessary further modification in due course.

The Commission also publishes from time to time Practice and Guidance Notes containing advice on particular points which have been drawn to its attention. A list of the current Practice, Guidance and other Notes is given at Annex A.

5. Finally a note on presentation. It is hoped that the Code will be helpful not only to those for whom the Act requires it to be written but also to patients, their families, friends and others who support them. It has been drafted as far as possible with this aim in mind. Throughout the Code the Mental Health Act 1983 is referred to as "the Act". Where there is reference to sections of other Acts, the relevant Act is clearly indicated.

6. In accordance with the requirements of the Welsh Language Act, this publication is available in the Welsh Language. Details can be obtained from

Robert Booth or Dominic Worsey
PCH4
Welsh Office, Health and Social Work Service
Cathays Park
Cardiff CF1 3NQ
Telephone: Robert Booth 01222 823998
             Dominic Worsey 01222 823480

Guiding principles

1.1 The detailed guidance in the Code needs to be read in the light of the following broad principles, that people to whom the Act applies (including those being assessed for possible admission) should:

- receive recognition of their basic human rights under the European Convention on Human Rights (ECHR);
- be given respect for their qualities, abilities and diverse backgrounds as individuals and be assured that account will be taken of their age, gender, sexual orientation, social, ethnic, cultural and religious background, but that general assumptions will not be made on the basis of any one of these characteristics;
- have their needs taken fully into account, though it is recognised that, within available resources, it may not always be practicable to meet them in full;
- be given any necessary treatment or care in the least controlled and segregated facilities compatible with ensuring their own health or safety or the safety of other people;
- be treated and cared for in such a way as to promote to the greatest practicable degree their self determination and personal responsibility, consistent with their own needs and wishes;
- be discharged from detention or other powers provided by the Act as soon as it is clear that their application is no longer justified.

The Care Programme Approach and Care Management

1.2 The delivery of all mental health services is framed within the Care

Programme Approach (CPA) set out in Circular HC(90)23/LASSL(90)11, and in the Welsh Office Mental Illness Strategy (WHC(95)40). The CPA provides the framework for all patients, both in hospital and in the community, and Health Authorities, Trusts and Social Services Authorities are responsible for ensuring that the Act is always be applied within this context.

The key elements of the CPA are:

- systematic arrangements for assessing people's health and social care needs;
- the formulation of a care plan which addresses those needs;
- the appointment of a key worker to keep in close touch with the patient and monitor care;
- regular reviews and if need be, agreed changes to the care plan.

Similarly Social Services Authorities also have a responsibility to undertake assessments of individuals' social care needs and design care plans in accordance with care management procedures. These two systems should as far as possible be integrated.

Communicating with patients

1.3 As a general principle, it is the responsibility of staff to ensure that effective communication takes place between themselves and patients. All those involved in the assessment, treatment and care of patients should ensure that everything possible is done to overcome any barriers to communication that may exist.

1.4 Local and Health Authorities and Trusts should ensure that ASWs, doctors, nurses and others receive sufficient guidance in the use of interpreters and should make arrangements for there to be an easily accessible pool of trained interpreters. Authorities and Trusts should consider co-operating in making this provision.

1.5 Barriers to communication may be caused by any one of a number of reasons, e.g. the patient's first language is not English or he or she may have difficulty understanding technical terms and jargon; he or she may have a hearing or visual impairment or have difficulty reading. There may also be barriers to communication associated with the person's mental disorder, for example, the patient may lack mental capacity.

1.6 Staff need to be aware of how communication difficulties affect each patient individually so that they can address the needs of patients in ways that best suit them. This will require patience and sensitivity. Specialist help should always be made available to staff as required, either from within the hospital itself, or from the local social services authority or a voluntary organisation. The patient's relatives or friends should not normally be used as an intermediary or interpreter. When the need arises, staff should make every attempt to identify interpreters who match the patient in gender, religion, dialect, and as closely as possible in age.

1.7 It will at times be necessary to convey the same information on a number of different occasions and frequently check that the patient has fully understood it. Information given to a patient who is unwell may need to be repeated when they have improved.

Confidentiality

1.8 Managers and staff in all Trusts, Authorities, Mental Nursing Homes, Social Services Departments and other organisations which provide services for patients should be familiar with the Department of Health (DH) Guidance on confidentiality (*The Protection and Use of Patient Information, Department of Health 1996, HSG(96)18*). Ordinarily, information about a patient should not be disclosed without the patient's consent. Occasionally it may be necessary to pass on particular information to professionals or others in the public interest, for instance where personal health or safety is at risk. Any such disclosure should be in accordance with the principles set out in the Guidance *(see also Building Bridges (para 1.5), Department of Health, February 1996, and guidance on the power to disclose information under section 115 of the Crime and Disorder Act, Home Office, 1998).*

Victims

1.9 Where a patient detained under Part III of the Act is both competent and willing to agree to the disclosure of specified information about his or her care, this should be encouraged to enable victims and victims' families to be informed about progress. It can be important to a patient's rehabilitation that victims understand what has been achieved in terms of modifying offending behaviour. Disclosure of such information also serves to reduce the danger of harmful confrontations after a discharge of which victims were unaware. Without prejudice to a patient's right to confidentiality, care teams should be ready to discuss with him or her the benefits of enabling some information to be given by professionals to victims, within the spirit of the *Victim's Charter (Home Office, 1996)*. The patient's agreement to do so must be freely given and he or she will need to understand the implications of agreeing to information being given to the victim(s). Care must be taken not to exert any pressure on the patients or this may bring into question the validity of the consent.

Information

1.10 The Hospital Managers have a statutory duty to give information to detained patients, and to their nearest relatives, unless the patient objects. A definition of the nearest relative under the Act is given at section 26. The Department of Health publishes leaflets about the information which should be given to detained patients.

1.11 All patients, including those subject to guardianship, should be given full information, both verbally and in writing, to help them understand why they are in hospital, or subject to guardianship, and the care and treatment they will be given. Informal patients who are capable of expressing consent should be told that they may leave at any time. Where mentally incapacitated patients have been admitted informally their position should be explained to them as far as possible and their close relative, carer or advocate should be kept informed about the arrangements for their care.

1.12 Information should be clearly displayed on ward notice boards and in reception areas. All patients should be given admission booklets, information about the Mental Health Act Commission and complaints leaflets for the Hospital, Trust and local Social Services Department. More details on the giving of information is in Chapter 14.

1.13 Authorities and Trusts should keep records of the ethnicity of all patients admitted under the Act. The NHS Executive's Information Management Group guidance *Collecting ethnic group data for admitted patient care - implementation guidance and training material* (*Department of Health 1994*) should be followed. The Department of Health's standard ethnicity codes should be used, namely:

0 White

1 Black Caribbean

2 Black African

3 Black other

4 Indian

5 Pakistani

6 Bangladesh

7 Chinese

8 Any other

9 Not given

and should establish a system to monitor admissions by race and sex.

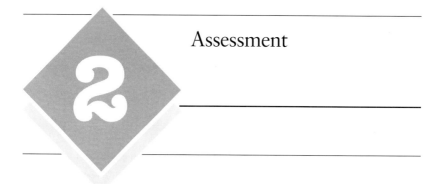

Assessment

General

2.1 This chapter is about the roles and responsibilities of ASWs and doctors when making assessments of the needs of a person with mental health problems, where the assessment may lead to an application for admission to hospital under the Act.

2.2 An individual should only be compulsorily admitted if the statutory criteria are met and other relevant factors have been considered as set out in para 2.6 below. A decision *not* to apply for admission under the Act should be supported, where necessary, by an alternative framework of care and/or treatment. The decision should also be clearly recorded in the patient's medical notes.

2.3 Doctors and ASWs undertaking assessments need to apply professional judgment, and reach decisions independently of each other but in a framework of co-operation and mutual support. Good working relationships require knowledge and understanding by the members of each profession of the other's distinct role and responsibilities. Unless there are good reasons for undertaking separate assessments, assessments should be carried out jointly by the ASW and doctor(s). It is essential that at least one of the doctors undertaking the medical assessment discusses the patient with the applicant (ASW or nearest relative) and desirable for both of them to do this.

2.4 Everyone involved in assessment should be alert to the need to provide support for colleagues, especially where there is a risk of the patient causing physical harm. Staff should be aware of circumstances where the police should be called to provide assistance, and how to use that assistance to minimise the risk of violence.

The objective of assessment under the Act

2.5 All those assessing for possible admission under the Act should ensure that:

- they take all relevant factors into account;
- they consider appropriate alternatives to compulsory admission;
- they comply with the legal requirements of the Act.

The factors to be taken into account at assessment

2.6 A patient may be compulsorily admitted under the Act where this is necessary:

- in the interests of his or her own health, <u>or</u>
- in the interests of his or her own safety, <u>or</u>
- for the protection of other people.

Only one of the above grounds needs to be satisfied (*in addition to those relating to the patient's mental disorder*). However, a patient may only be admitted for treatment under section 3 if the treatment cannot be provided unless he or she is detained under the section. In judging whether compulsory admission is appropriate, those concerned should consider not only the statutory criteria but should also take account of:

- the guiding principles in Chapter 1
- the patient's wishes and view of his or her own needs;
- the patient's social and family circumstances;
- the nature of the illness/behaviour disorder and its course;
- what may be known about the patient by his or her nearest relative, any other relatives or friends and professionals involved, assessing in particular how reliable this information is;
- other forms of care or treatment including, where relevant, consideration of whether the patient would be willing to accept

medical treatment in hospital informally or as an out-patient and of whether guardianship would be appropriate (see chapter 13);

- the needs of the patient's family or others with whom he or she lives;
- the need for others to be protected from the patient;
- the burden on those close to the patient of a decision not to admit under the Act.

Ordinarily only then should the applicant (in consultation with other professionals) judge whether the criteria stipulated in any of the admission sections are satisfied, and take the decision accordingly. In certain circumstances the urgency of the situation may curtail detailed consideration of all these factors.

Informal admission

2.7 Where admission to hospital is considered necessary and the patient is willing to be admitted informally this should in general be arranged. Compulsory admission powers should only be exercised in the last resort. Informal admission is usually appropriate when a mentally capable patient consents to admission, but not if detention is necessary because of the danger the patient presents to him or herself or others. Compulsory admission should be considered where a mentally capable patient's current medical state, together with reliable evidence of past experience, indicates a strong likelihood that he or she will have a change of mind about informal admission prior to actually being admitted to hospital, with a resulting risk to their health or safety or to the safety of other people.

2.8 If at the time of admission, the patient is mentally incapable of consent, but does not object to entering hospital and receiving care or treatment, admission should be informal[1] (see paras 15.9-15.10 for assessment of capacity and 15.18-15.22 for the treatment of mentally incapacitated patients). The decision to admit a mentally incapacitated patient informally should be made by the doctor in charge of the patient's treatment in accordance with what is in the patient's best interests and is justifiable on the basis of the common law doctrine of neces-

---

[1] R v Bournewood Community and Mental Health NHS Trust ex parte L [1998] 3 ALL ER 289

sity (see para 15.21). If a patient lacks capacity at the time of an assessment or review, it is particularly important that both clinical and social care requirements are considered, and that account is taken of the patient's ascertainable wishes and feelings and the views of their immediate relatives and carers on what would be in the patient's best interests.

Protection of others

2.9 In considering the protection of others (see sections 2(2)(b) and 3(2)(c) of the Act) it is essential to assess both the nature and likelihood of risk and the level of risk others are entitled to be protected from, taking into account:

- reliability of evidence including any relevant details of the patient's clinical history and past behaviour including contact with other agencies;
- the degree of risk and its nature. A risk of physical harm, or serious persistent psychological harm, to others is an indicator of the need for compulsory admission;
- the willingness and ability to cope with the risk, by those with whom the patient lives, and whether there are alternative options available for managing the risk.

The health of the patient

2.10 A patient may be admitted under sections 2 or 3 solely in the interests of his or her own health or safety even if there is no risk to other people. Those assessing the patient must consider:

- any evidence suggesting that the patient's mental health will deteriorate if he or she does not receive treatment;
- the reliability of such evidence which may include the known history of the individual's mental disorder;
- the views of the patient and of any relatives or close friends, especially those living with the patient, about the likely course of the illness and the possibility of it improving;
- the impact that any future deterioration or lack of improvement would have on relatives or close friends, especially those living with

the patient, including an assessment of their ability and willingness to cope;

- whether there are other methods of coping with the expected deterioration or lack of improvement.

Individual professional responsibility - the Approved Social Worker

2.11 It is important to emphasise that an ASW assessing a patient for possible admission under the Act has overall responsibility for co-ordinating the process of assessment and, where he or she decides to make an application, for implementing that decision. The ASW must, at the start of the assessment, identify him or herself to the person, members of the family or friends present and the other professionals involved in the assessment. They should explain in clear terms the ASW's own role and the purpose of the visit, and ensure that the other professionals have explained their roles. ASWs should carry with them at all times documents identifying them as ASWs.

2.12 The ASW must interview the patient in a 'suitable manner', taking account of the guiding principles in Chapter 1:

a. It is not desirable for a patient to be interviewed through a closed door or window except where there is serious risk to other people. Where there is no immediate risk of physical danger to the patient or to others, powers in the Act to secure access (section 135) should be used.

b. Where the patient is subject to the effects of sedative medication, or the short-term effects of drugs or alcohol, the ASW should consult with the doctor(s) and, unless it is not possible because of the patient's disturbed behaviour and the urgency of the case, either wait until, or arrange to return when, the effects have abated before interviewing the patient. If it is not realistic, or the risk indicates that it would not be appropriate to wait, the assessment will have to be based on whatever information the ASW can obtain from all reliable sources. This should be made clear in the ASW's report.

2.13 The patient should ordinarily be given the opportunity of speaking to the ASW alone but if the ASW has reason to fear physical harm, he or she should insist that another professional be present. If the patient wants or needs another person (for example a friend, relative or an advocate) to be present during the assessment and any subsequent action that may be taken, then ordinarily the ASW should assist in securing that person's attendance unless the urgency of the case or some other reason makes it inappropriate to do so. Deaf or hearing impaired patients may feel more confident with a friend or advocate who is also deaf or hearing impaired.

2.14 The ASW must attempt to identify the patient's nearest relative as defined in section 26 of the Act *(see paras 62-63 of the Memorandum)*. It is important to remember that the nearest relative for the purposes of the Act may not be the same person as the patient's "next of kin", and also that the identity of the nearest relative is liable to change with the passage of time. The ASW must then ensure that the statutory obligations with respect to the nearest relative set out in section 11 of the Act are fulfilled. In addition, the ASW should where possible:

a. ascertain the nearest relative's views about both the patient's needs and the relative's own needs in relation to the patient;

b. inform the nearest relative of the reasons for considering an application for admission under the Act and the effects of making such an application.

Applications under section 2

2.15 It is a statutory requirement to take such steps as are practicable to inform the nearest relative about an application for admission under section 2 and of their power of discharge (section 11(3)). If the ASW has been unable to inform the nearest relative before the patient's admission, he or she should notify the hospital as soon as this has been done.

Applications under section 3

2.16 Consultation by the ASW with the nearest relative about possible application for admission under section 3 or reception into guardianship is a statutory requirement unless it is not reasonably practicable or would involve unreasonable delay (section 11(4)). Circumstances in which the nearest relative need not be informed or consulted include those where the ASW cannot obtain sufficient information to establish the identity or location of the nearest relative or where to do so would require an excessive amount of investigation. Practicability refers to the availability of the nearest relative and not to the appropriateness of informing or consulting the person concerned. If the ASW has been unable to consult the nearest relative before making an application for admission for treatment (section 3) he or she should persist in seeking to contact the nearest relative so as to inform the latter of his or her powers to discharge the patient under section 23. The ASW should inform the hospital as soon as this has been done.

Delegation of nearest relative's functions

2.17 If the nearest relative would find it difficult to undertake the functions defined in the Act, or is reluctant for any reason to do this, regulation 14[2] allows him or her to delegate those functions to another person. ASWs should consider proposing this in appropriate cases.

2.18 If the nearest relative objects to an application being made for admission for treatment or reception into guardianship it cannot proceed at that time. If, because of the urgency of the case, and the risks of not taking forward the application immediately, it is thought necessary to proceed with the application, the ASW will then need to consider applying to the county court for the nearest relative's 'displacement' (section 29), and Local Authorities must provide proper assistance, especially legal assistance, in such cases. It is desirable for social services authorities to provide clear practical guidance on the procedures, and this should be discussed with the relevant county courts.

2.19 In so far as the urgency of the case allows, an ASW who is the applicant for the admission of a patient to hospital should consult with other relevant relatives and should take their views into account.

2.20 The ASW should consult wherever possible with others who have been involved with the patient's care in the statutory, voluntary or independent services. Deaf patients may be known to one of the specialist hospital units for mental health and deafness.

---

[2] Mental Health (Hospital, Guardianship and Consent to Treatment) Regulations 1983

2.21 Having decided whether or not to make an application for admission the ASW should tell (with reasons):

- the patient;
- the patient's nearest relative (whenever practicable);
- the doctor(s) involved in the assessment;
- the key worker, if the patient is on CPA;
- the patient's GP, if he or she was not involved in the assessment.

When an application for admission is to be made the ASW should plan how the patient is to be conveyed to hospital and take steps to make the necessary arrangements (see Chapter 11).

Individual professional responsibility - the doctor

2.22 The doctor should:

a. decide whether the patient is suffering from mental disorder within the meaning of the Act (section 1) and assess its seriousness and the need for further assessment and/or medical treatment in hospital;

b. consider the factors set out in para 2.6, and discuss them with the applicant and the other doctor involved;

c. specifically address the legal criteria for admission under the Act and, if satisfied that they are met, provide a recommendation setting out those aspects of the patient's symptoms and behaviour on which that conclusion is based;

d. ensure that, where there is to be an application for admission, a hospital bed will be available.

Medical examination

2.23 A proper medical examination requires:

- direct personal examination of the patient's mental state;
- consideration of all available relevant medical information including that in the possession of others, professional or non-professional;
- that the guiding principles in Chapter 1 are taken into account.

2.24 If direct access to the patient is not immediately possible, and it is not desirable to postpone the examination in order to negotiate access, consideration should be given to calling the police in order to exercise their lawful power of entry set out in the Act (section 135).

2.25 It may not always be practicable for the patient to be examined by both doctors at the same time; but they should always discuss the patient with each other.

2.26 It is desirable for both doctors to discuss the patient with the applicant. It is essential for at least one of them to do so (see para 2.3).

Joint medical recommendations

2.27 Joint medical recommendations forms (3 and 10) should only be used where the patient has been jointly examined by two doctors. It is desirable that they are completed and signed by both doctors at the same time.

2.28 In all other circumstances separate recommendation forms should be used (forms 4 and 11).

The second medical recommendation

2.29 Unless there are exceptional circumstances, the second medical recommendation should be provided by a doctor with previous acquaintance with the patient (that is, one who knows the patient personally in his or her professional capacity). This should be the case even when the 'approved' doctor (who is, for example, a hospital-based consultant) already knows the patient. Where this is not possible (for example the patient is not registered with a GP) it is desirable for the second medical recommendation to be provided by an 'approved' doctor (see paras 2.41 and 2.42).

2.30 Where a Trust manages two or more hospitals which are in different places and have different names one of the two doctors making the medical recommendations may be on the staff of one hospital and the second doctor may be on the staff of one of the other hospitals.

A decision not to apply for admission

2.31 Most compulsory admissions require prompt action to be taken. It should be remembered that the ASW has up to 14 days from having personally seen the patient to complete an application for admission under section 2 or 3. The duly completed application and the medical recommendations provide the ASW with the authority to convey the patient to hospital and, in the case of an application for admission under section 2 or 3, such authority lasts for 14 days from the date when the patient was last examined by a doctor with a view to making a recommendation for his or her admission. Where a decision not to apply for a patient's compulsory admission is taken, the ASW must decide how to implement those actions (if any) which his or her assessment indicates are necessary to meet the needs of the patient including, for example, referral to other social workers or services within the social services department. It is particularly important that any keyworker concerned with the patient's care be fully involved in the taking of such decisions. The professionals must ensure that they, the patient and (with the patient's consent except where section 13(4) applies) the patient's nearest relative and any other closely connected relatives have a clear understanding of any alternative arrangements. Such arrangements and any plans for reviewing them must be recorded in writing and copies made available to all those who need them (subject to the patient's right to confidentiality).

2.32 The ASW must discuss with the patient's nearest relative the reasons for not making an application and should advise the nearest relative of his or her right to do this. If the nearest relative wishes to pursue this the ASW should suggest that he or she consult with the doctors. Where the ASW has carried out an assessment at the request of the nearest relative (section 13(4)) the reasons for not applying for the patient's admission must be given to the nearest relative in writing. Such a letter should contain sufficient details to enable the nearest relative to understand the decision whilst at the same time preserving the patient's right to confidentiality.

Particular practice issues - disagreements

2.33 Sometimes there will be differences of opinion between assessing professionals. There is nothing wrong with disagreements: handled properly these offer an opportunity to safeguard the interests of the patient by widening the discussion on the best way of meeting his or her needs. Doctors and ASWs should be ready to consult colleagues (especially keyworkers and other community care staff involved with the patient's care) while retaining for themselves the final responsibility. Where disagreements do occur, professionals should ensure that they discuss these with each other.

2.34 Where there is an unresolved dispute about an application for admission, it is essential that the professionals do not abandon the patient and the family. Rather, they should explore and agree an alternative plan, if necessary on a temporary basis, and ensure that the family is kept informed. Such a plan and the arrangements for reviewing it should be recorded in writing and copies made available to all those who need it (subject to the patient's right to confidentiality).

The choice of applicant for admission

2.35 The ASW is usually the right applicant, bearing in mind professional training, knowledge of the legislation and of local resources, together with the potential adverse effect that an application by the nearest relative might have on the latter's relationship with the patient. The doctor should therefore advise the nearest relative that it is preferable for an ASW to make an assessment of the need for a patient to be admitted under the Act, and for the ASW to make the application. When reasonably practicable the doctor should, however, advise the nearest relative of the rights set out in section 13(4) (see para 2.38) and of his or her right to make an application.

2.36 The doctor should never advise the nearest relative to make an application in order to avoid involving an ASW in an assessment.

Agency responsibilities - the Local Authority

2.37 A nearest relative should not be put in the position of having to make an application for admission under the Act because it is not possible for an ASW to attend for assessment. Subject to resources, local authorities should provide a 24 hour ASW service to ensure that this does not happen.

Section 13 (4)

2.38 Local Authorities are required, if requested by a nearest relative, to direct an ASW to make an assessment and:

a. should have explicit policies on how to respond to repeated requests for assessment where the condition of a patient has not changed significantly;

b. should give guidance to ASWs as to whether nearest relative requests can be accepted by way of GPs or other professions. (Such requests should certainly be accepted provided the GP or other professional has been so authorised by the nearest relative.)

Emergencies out of hours etc

2.39 Arrangements should be made to ensure that information about applications is passed to professional colleagues who are next on duty. For example, where an application for admission is not immediately necessary but might be in the future, the necessary arrangements could be made for an ASW to attend the next day.

Agency responsibilities - the Health Authority

Doctors approved under section 12

2.40 The Secretary of State has delegated to Health Authorities the task of approving medical practitioners under section 12(2).

2.41 Health Authorities should:

a. take active steps to encourage sufficient doctors, including GPs and those working in the Health Care Service for Prisoners, to apply for approval;

b. seek to ensure a 24 hour on-call rota of approved doctors sufficient to cover the area;

c. maintain a regularly updated list of approved doctors which indicates how each approved doctor can be contacted and the hours that he or she is available;

d. ensure that the up-to-date list of approved doctors and details of the 24 hour on-call rota are circulated to all concerned parties including GPs, mental health centres and social services.

2.42 Authorities and Trusts should consider including in the job description for new consultant psychiatrists with a responsibility for providing a catchment area service obligations to become approved under section 12 of the Act, to keep such approval up-to-date and to participate in the 24 hour on-call approved doctors' rota.

Health Authorities/Trusts/Local Authorities

2.43 Good practice requires that Health Authorities, Trusts and local Social Services Authorities should co-operate in ensuring that regular meetings take place between professionals involved in mental health assessments in order to promote understanding, and to provide a forum for clarification of their respective roles and responsibilities. Professionals should also keep in mind the interface with the criminal justice agencies, including the probation service and the police.

Part III of the Act - patients concerned with criminal proceedings

Assessment prior to possible admission

General

3.1 People subject to criminal proceedings have the same right to psychiatric assessment and treatment as other citizens. Any person who is in police or prison custody, who is in need of medical treatment for mental disorder which can only be satisfactorily given in a hospital (or mental nursing home) as defined by the Act, should be admitted to such a hospital. If criminal proceedings are discontinued it may be appropriate for the police to alert the relevant local social services department to allow them to consider whether an application under Part II of the Act would be appropriate.

3.2 All professionals involved in the operation of Part III of the Act should remember:

a.   that mentally disordered people in police or prison custody may be very vulnerable. The risk of suicide or other self destructive behaviour should be of special concern;

b.   that a prison health care centre is not a hospital within the meaning of the Act. Comprehensive treatment facilities are rarely available, and the provisions of Part IV of the Act do not apply.

Individual professional responsibilities

3.3 All professionals concerned with the operation of Part III of the Act should be familiar with:

•   the relevant provisions of the Act *[see paras 141-211 of the Memorandum]*;

- Home Office and Department of Health guidance relating to mentally disordered offenders including Home Office Circular 12/95;
- their own professional responsibilities and those of other disciplines and authorities and agencies;
- available facilities and services.

Agency responsibilities

3.4 Health Authorities should:

a. be able to provide in response to a request from a court under section 39 of the Act, or other proper requests, up-to-date and full information on the range of facilities that would be available for a potential patient from their area, including secure facilities [see para 173 of the Memorandum] ;

b. appoint a named person to respond to requests for information.

3.5 Section 39A which was introduced under sections 27 of the Criminal Justice Act 1991 requires a local social services authority to inform the court if requested, if it or any other person is willing to receive the offender into guardianship and how the guardian's powers would be exercised.

3.6 Local Authorities should appoint a named person to respond to requests from the courts about mental health services provided in the community including guardianship.

Assessment by a doctor

3.7 A doctor who is asked to provide an opinion in relation to a possible admission under Part lll of the Act should:

a. identify him or herself to the person being assessed, explain who has requested the report and the limits of confidentiality in relation to the report, including that the data and the opinion could be relevant not only to medical disposal by the Court but also to the imposition of a punitive sentence, or to its length (see para 3.12);

b. request relevant pre-sentence reports, the Inmate Medical Record, if there is one, previous psychiatric reports as well as relevant documentation regarding the alleged offence. If any of this information is not available, the doctor's report should say so clearly.

The report should, where possible, be prepared by a doctor who has previously treated the patient. The doctor, or one of them if two doctors are preparing reports, should have access to a bed or take responsibility for referring the case to another doctor who does (see para 3.18).

3.8 The doctor should where possible identify and access other independent sources of information about the person's previous history (including convictions), including information from GP records, previous psychiatric treatment and patterns of behaviour.

3.9 Assessment for admission of the patient is the responsibility of the doctor but other members of the clinical team who would be involved with the person's care and treatment should also be consulted. A nursing assessment should usually be undertaken if admission to hospital is likely to be recommended. The doctor should also contact the person who is preparing a pre-sentence report, especially if psychiatric treatment is recommended as a condition of a probation order.

3.10 In cases where the doctor cannot state with confidence at the time of sentencing whether admission to hospital will be beneficial, he or she should consider recommending an interim hospital order under section 38 of the Act. This order provides for the person to be admitted to hospital for up to 12 weeks (which may be extended for further periods of up to 28 days to a maximum total period of 12 months) so that recommendations as to treatability and the appropriateness of continuing treatment in hospital can be fully informed.

Reports to the court

3.11 The weight of the clinical opinion is particularly important in helping courts to determine the sentence to be passed. In the case of patients subject to criminal proceedings the doctor's report should set out clearly:

a. the data on which the report is based;

b. how this relates to the opinion given;

c. where relevant, how the opinion may relate to any medical condition defence, or other trial issue;

d. factors relating to the presence of mental disorder that may affect the risk that the patient poses to him or herself, or to others, including risk of re-offending; and

e. if admission to hospital is recommended, what, if any, special treatment or security is required and how this would be addressed.

The report should not comment on guilt or innocence.

3.12 When sentencing mentally disordered offenders the court is bound by the requirement in section 4 of the Criminal Justice Act 1991 to consider any information before it which relates to the patient's mental condition. Except where the offence is one for which the law requires a life sentence the court must, before passing sentence, consider the effect of a custodial sentence on the offender's mental disorder and on the treatment which may be available for it.

3.13 A medical report will be of crucial importance in determining whether or not a sentence of life imprisonment should be imposed where this is not mandatory.

3.14 In a report submitted to the court it may be appropriate to include recommendations on the disposal of the case including any need for a further report in the event of conviction. In making recommendations for disposal the doctor should consider the longer term, as well as immediate, consequences. Factors to be taken into account include:

a. whether the court may wish to make a hospital order subject to special restrictions [see paras 162-164 of the Memorandum];

b. whether, for restricted patients, the order should designate admission to a named unit within the hospital.

3.15 The power of the courts to order admission to a named unit was introduced by the Crime (Sentences) Act 1997 to enable the court or the Home Secretary to specify a level of security in which the patient needs to be detained. A named hospital unit can be any part of a hospital which is treated as a separate unit. It will be for the court to define what is meant in each case where it makes use of the power. Admission to a named unit will mean the Home Secretary's consent will be required for any leave or transfer from the named unit, whether the transfer is to another part of the same hospital or to another hospital.

3.16 The need to consider the longer term implications of a recommended disposal is particularly important following the introduction of powers under section 45A of the Act (introduced under the Crime (Sentences) Act 1997). This provides a new option, if the offender is diagnosed as suffering from psychopathic disorder within the meaning of section 1 of the Act (with or without an additional category of mental disorder), for the court to attach a hospital direction and limitation direction to a prison sentence. Where either a hospital order under section 37 or a prison sentence with a hospital direction under section 45A is available to the court the choice rests with the court. The making of a hospital direction and a limitation direction will mean that from the start of his or her sentence the offender will be managed in hospital as if he or she was a transferred prisoner (under section 47 and 49). Thereafter the responsible medical officer (rmo) will have the option of seeking the patient's transfer to prison at any time before his or her release date if no further treatment is likely to be beneficial.

3.17 It is a matter for the discretion of the court whether to make a hospital order subject to restrictions. A hospital direction must always be accompanied by a limitation direction which applies restrictions. It is also for the courts to decide whether to name a hospital unit.

Availability of places

3.18 If the doctor has concluded that the person needs treatment in hospital but is not able to identify a suitable facility where the person could be admitted immediately, he or she should consider seeking advice from the NHS forensic mental health service or learning disability services for the person's home area. Once advice has been sought, written details of the type of provision required should be sent to the responsible Health Authority, together with relevant supporting information which the authority will need in order to discharge their responsibilities.

Requests for ASW assessment

3.19 When an ASW is requested to undertake an assessment in prison or court with a view to making an application for admission under section 2 or section 3 or guardianship, he or she must be given as much notice as possible, and time and facilities to interview the prisoner. The ASW should be given access to the pre-sentence report and any other relevant records and reports.

Transfer of prisoners to hospital

3.20 The need for in-patient treatment for a prisoner should be identified and acted upon quickly and contact made immediately between the prison doctor and the hospital doctor. The Home Office Mental Health Unit should be informed as soon as the statutory requirements for transfer are in place so that consideration can be given to issuing a direction under the Home Secretary's powers. Supporting reports should take account of the guidance on reports to the courts in paras 3.11 and 3.14 above.

3.21 The transfer of a prisoner to hospital under the Act should take place as soon as possible after the need has been identified. A transfer close to the expected date of release may be seen by the prisoner as being primarily intended to extend detention and result in an unco-operative attitude towards treatment.

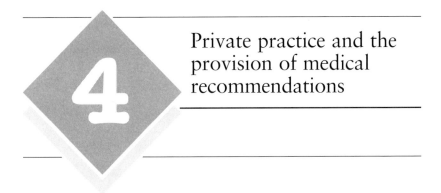

Private practice and the provision of medical recommendations

4.1 The Act restricts the provision of medical recommendations by certain categories of doctor in private practice. Thus:

a. where an individual is to be admitted to a mental nursing home or as a private patient to a hospital, neither medical recommendation can be provided by a doctor on the staff of the hospital or mental nursing home (section 12(3));

b. no medical recommendation can be provided by a doctor who receives, or has an interest in the receipt of, any payment made on account of the maintenance of the patient (section 12(5)(d)).

4.2 It is the personal responsibility of any doctor providing a medical recommendation to ensure that he or she is complying with these legal requirements; if in doubt legal advice must be sought.

4.3 It is undesirable for a doctor to provide a recommendation where he or she will receive payment from the patient (or a relative or friend or an insurance company) for medical services to be provided after he or she has been admitted as a private patient to a hospital or mental nursing home.

4.4 If there could be any suspicion (however unjustified) that a doctor providing a medical recommendation is doing so for pecuniary advantage, then arrangements should be made for another doctor to make the recommendation.

4.5 Where the patient is currently receiving treatment from a doctor that doctor should be consulted by the doctor(s) providing the medical recommendation.

Section 2 or section 3?

The choice

5.1 Which admission section should be used? Professional judgment must be applied to the criteria in each section and only when this has been done can a decision be reached as to which, if either, section applies. Detention under section 3 can last for any period of time, and need not last its full course.

5.2 **Section 2 pointers:**

a. the diagnosis and prognosis of a patient's condition is unclear;

b. a need to carry out an in-patient assessment in order to formulate a treatment plan;

c. a judgment is needed as to whether the patient will accept treatment on a voluntary basis following admission;

d. a judgment has to be made as to whether a particular treatment proposal, which can only be administered to the patient under Part IV of the Act, is likely to be effective;

e. the condition of a patient who has already been assessed, and who has been previously admitted compulsorily under the Act, is judged to have changed since the previous admission and further assessment is needed;

f. the patient has not previously been admitted to hospital either compulsorily or informally and has not been in regular contact with the specialist psychiatric services.

5.3 Section 3 pointers:

a. the patient is considered to need compulsory admission for the treatment of a mental disorder which is already known to his clinical team, and has been assessed in the recent past by that team. In these circumstances it may be right to use section 3 even where the patient has not previously been admitted as an in-patient;

b. the patient is detained under section 2 and assessment indicates a need for treatment under the Act for a period beyond the 28 day detention under section 2. In such circumstances an application for detention under section 3 should be made at the earliest opportunity and should not be delayed until the end of section 2 detention. The change in detention status from section 2 to section 3 will not deprive the patient of a Mental Health Review Tribunal hearing if the change takes place after a valid application has been made to the Tribunal but before that application has been heard. The patient's rights to apply for a Tribunal under section 66(1)(b) in the first period of detention after his change of status are unaffected.

5.4 Decisions should not be influenced by the possibility that:

a. a proposed treatment to be administered under the Act will last less than 28 days;

b. a patient detained under section 2 will get quicker access to a Mental Health Review Tribunal than one detained under section 3;

c. after-care under supervision will only be available if the patient has been admitted under section 3 (see Chapter 27). The use of section 3 must be justified by the patient's need to be admitted for treatment under the terms of that section, not considerations about what is to happen after his or her eventual discharge;

d. a patient's nearest relative objects to admission under section 3.

5.5 If the nearest relative unreasonably objects to admission under section 3 an application should be made to the county court under section 29 of the Act for the functions of the nearest relative to be transferred to the local Social Services Authority or another person. A further section 2 application cannot be made if the patient is already in hospital following admission under section 2[3]. The section 29 application should be made as soon as it is clear that the patient will need to be detained under section 3 and that the nearest relative unreasonably objects to this.

---

[3] R v Wilson ex parte W [1996] COD 42

Admission for assessment in an emergency (section 4)

(Para 24 of the Memorandum)

General

6.1 Application for admission for assessment under section 4 should be made only when:

a. the criteria for admission for assessment are met (see para 5.2); and

b. the matter is of urgent necessity and there is not enough time to get a second medical recommendation.

6.2 Section 4 should be used only in a genuine emergency, never for administrative convenience. 'Second doctors' should be available to assist with assessments prior to admission.

Admission

6.3 An emergency arises where those involved cannot cope with the mental state or behaviour of the patient. To be satisfied that an emergency has arisen, there must be evidence of:

• an immediate and significant risk of mental or physical harm to the patient or to others; and/or

• the danger of serious harm to property; and/or

• the need for physical restraint of the patient.

6.4 Patients should not be admitted under section 4 rather than section 2 because it is more convenient for the second doctor to examine the patient in, rather than outside, hospital. Those assessing an individual's need must be able to secure the attendance within a reasonable time of a second doctor and in particular an approved doctor.

6.5 If the ASW is considering an application for admission and no second doctor is available, he or she should discuss the case with the doctor providing the recommendation and seek to resolve the problem. If this is not possible he or she should have access to an officer in the local Social Services Authority who is sufficiently senior to take up the matter with the Health Authority or Trust. The ASW's Local Authority should make it clear that the ASW in these circumstances is under an obligation to report the matter in this way.

6.6 Hospital Managers should monitor the use of section 4 and seek to ensure that second doctors are available to visit a patient within a reasonable time after being so requested.

6.7 If a patient is admitted under section 4 an appropriate second doctor should examine him or her as soon as possible after admission, to decide whether the patient should be detained under section 2.

Part III of the Act - patients admitted from prison or remand centre

Admission

7.1 The following documents should be sent from the prison or remand centre to the hospital at the time of transfer:

- an up-to-date medical report including details of medication
- a report from Prison Health Care staff covering the patient's day-to-day care and management including risk factors
- any relevant pre-sentence reports prepared by the probation service.

It is important that all information is made available to the patient's rmo and other professional staff concerned.

Restricted patients

7.2 When a person is transferred from prison to hospital under sections 47 or 48 as a restricted patient, it is the responsibility of the Hospital Managers and the rmo to ensure that the patient has received, and as far as possible, understood the letter from the Home Office explaining the roles of Hospital Managers and rmos in relation to restricted patients. Patients should also be given patient leaflets 18 and 20 which explain prison/hospital transfers under these sections.

Patients on remand/subject to an interim hospital order

7.3 For patients detained under sections 35, 36, 37 and 38 it is the court's responsibility to organise appropriate transport from the court to the receiving hospital.

Doctor's holding power (section 5(2))

(Paras 25-27 of the Memorandum)

8.1 Good practice depends upon:

a. the professionals involved in implementing the holding power (and in particular the doctor invoking it) correctly understanding the power and its purpose;

b. the Health Authority, Trust and local Social Services Authority making necessary arrangements and agreeing performance standards to ensure that when the power is used, the patient is assessed as quickly as possible for possible admission under the Act by an ASW and doctors; and

c. the Hospital Managers monitoring the use of the power.

Nature of the power

8.2 The power, which authorises the detention of the patient for up to 72 hours, can be used only where the doctor in charge of the treatment of an informal in-patient, or that doctor's nominated deputy, concludes that an application for admission under one of the relevant sections of the Act is appropriate. For this purpose, informal in-patients include those being treated for physical disorders who need treatment for a mental disorder. The period of detention commences at the moment the doctor's report (form 12) is delivered to the Hospital Managers, or someone authorised to receive such a report on their behalf.

8.3 Detention under section 5(2) will end immediately where:

a. an assessment for admission under section 2 or 3 is made and a decision is taken not to make an application for detention under section 2 or 3;

b. the doctor decides that no assessment for possible detention under section 2 or 3 needs to be carried out.

The patient should be informed that he or she is no longer detained under the doctor's holding power. The decision, the reasons for it, and its time should be recorded preferably on a form prepared for the purpose. The power cannot be renewed, but circumstances may arise where, subsequent to its use and the patient's reversion to informal status, its use can be considered again.

8.4 For the purposes of section 5(2), informal patients are usually voluntary patients, that is, those who have the capacity to consent and who consent to enter hospital for in-patient treatment. Patients who lack the capacity to consent but do not object to admission for treatment may also be informal patients (see para 2.8). The section cannot be used for an out-patient attending a hospital's accident and emergency department. Admission procedures should not be implemented with the sole intention of then using the power in section 5(2).

8.5 Where a report under section 5(2) is provided in relation to a patient under the care of a consultant other than a psychiatrist, the doctor invoking the power should make immediate contact with a psychiatrist.

8.6 Where a patient is receiving treatment for a physical disorder and a mental disorder for the purposes of section 5(2) the consultant psychiatrist is the doctor in charge of treatment.

Information

8.7 Where a patient is detained under section 5(2), the Hospital Managers must ensure that the requirements of section 132 to give information are fulfilled (see Chapter 14).

Treatment

8.8 Part IV of the Act does not apply to a patient detained under section 5(2). A patient detained under Section 5(2) who has the capacity to consent can only be treated if he or she consents to the treatment. A patient who lacks capacity to consent may be treated under the common law doctrine of necessity in their own best interests (see Chapter 15).

The doctor's role

8.9 Section 5(2) should only be used if at the time it is not possible or safe to use section 2, 3 or 4. Section 5(2) is not an admission section under the Act.

8.10 The patient's doctor, or nominated deputy, should only use the power immediately after having personally examined the patient. The doctor should not complete a section 5(2) form and leave it on the ward with instruction for others to submit it to the Hospital Managers if, in their view, the patient is about to leave.

Hospital Managers' responsibilities

8.11 The patient may only be detained when the doctor's section 5(2) report has been delivered to the Hospital Managers, or somebody authorised to receive it on their behalf. It is therefore important that there is no delay in delivering the report to the Hospital Managers and that sufficient staff are authorised to enable reports to be received at any time. The doctor or nominated deputy must always be aware of who the authorised person is.

Assessment for admission while a patient is 'held' under section 5(2)

8.12 All the normal procedures apply, including the use of either section 2 or section 3 if compulsory admission is thought necessary.

Nominated deputies - section 5(3)

8.13 The registered medical practitioner in charge of an in-patient's treatment may nominate a deputy to exercise section 5(2) powers during his or her absence from the hospital. That deputy will then act on his or her own responsibility and should be suitably experienced.

8.14 Some safeguards:

a. Where the nominated deputy is a junior doctor, the nominating doctor must be satisfied that the deputy has received sufficient guidance and training to carry out the function satisfactorily.

b. Wherever possible the nominated deputy must contact the nominating doctor or another consultant, where the nominated deputy is not a consultant, before using section 5(2). The nominated deputy should have easy access to the nominating doctor or the consultant psychiatrist on call.

c. Only registered medical practitioners who are consultant psychiatrists should nominate deputies.

d. The nominated deputy should report the use of section 5(2) to the nominator as soon as possible.

e. All relevant staff should know who is the nominated deputy for a particular patient.

8.15 It is unlawful for one nominated deputy to nominate another.

8.16 It is usual practice outside normal working hours for the nominated deputy to be the junior doctor on call for the admission wards. Where this occurs the nominating doctor is responsible for ensuring that all the doctors liable to be on duty are competent to act as the nominated deputy and that they are adequately trained, and that an individual doctor has been nominated for every duty period.

Transfer to other hospitals

8.17 It is not possible for patients detained under section 5(2) to be transferred to another hospital under section 19 (because they are not detained by virtue of an application made under Part II of the Act). Guidance on the implications of this, and on the circumstances in which such patients may be lawfully transferred, is given in the Mental Health Act Commission's Practice Note 3 (March 1994).

Nurse's holding power (section 5(4))

(Paras 28-29 of the Memorandum)

The power

9.1 A psychiatric emergency requires the urgent attendance of a doctor. In practice, a doctor may not be immediately available. This chapter sets out the circumstances in which a nurse of the "prescribed class"[4] may lawfully prevent an informal in-patient, receiving medical treatment for mental disorder, from leaving the hospital. The holding power may only be applied for up to 6 hours or until a doctor with the power to use section 5(2) in respect of the patient arrives, whichever is the earlier, and can only be used when the patient is still on the hospital premises. The holding power cannot be renewed. It is the personal decision of the nurse who cannot be instructed to exercise this power by anyone else. Part IV of the Act does not apply to patients detained under section 5(4).

Assessment before implementation

9.2 Before using the power the nurse should assess:

---

[4] Defined in the 1998 order as "a nurse registered in Part 3 (first level nurses trained in the nursing of persons suffering from mental illness) or Part 4 (second level nurses trained in the nursing of persons suffering from mental illness) or Part 5 (first level nurses trained in the nursing of person suffering from learning disabilities) or Part 6 (second level nurses trained in the nursing of persons suffering from learning disabilities) or Part 13 (nurses qualified following a course of preparation in mental health nursing) or Part 14 (nurses qualified following a course of preparation in learning disabilities nursing)" of the professional register established under the Nurses, Midwives and Health Visitors Act 1997.

a. the likely arrival time of the doctor as against the likely intention of the patient to leave. Most patients who express a wish to leave hospital can be persuaded to wait until a doctor arrives to discuss it further. Where this is not possible the nurse must try to predict the impact of any delay upon the patient;

b. the consequences of a patient leaving hospital immediately - the harm that might occur to the patient or others - taking into account:

- the patient's expressed intentions including the likelihood of the patient committing self-harm or suicide;

- any evidence of disordered thinking;

- the patient's current behaviour and in particular any changes in usual behaviour:

- the likelihood of the patient behaving in a violent manner;

- any recently received messages from relatives or friends;

- any recent disturbances on the ward;

- any relevant involvement of other patients;

c. the patient's known unpredictability and any other relevant information from other members of the multi-disciplinary team.

Acute emergencies

9.3 Normally assessment should precede action but in extreme circumstances it may be necessary to invoke the power without carrying out the proper assessment. The suddenness of the patient's determination to leave and the urgency with which the patient attempts to do so should alert the nurse to potentially serious consequences if the patient is successful in leaving.

Reports

9.4 The nurse entitled to use the power does so by completing form 13. This must be delivered to the Hospital Managers, or to an officer appointed by them, as soon as possible after completion. It is essential that:

a. the reasons for invoking the power are entered in the patient's nursing and medical notes;

b. a local incident report form is sent to the Hospital Managers;

c. details of any patients who remain subject to the power at the time of a shift change are given to staff coming on duty.

9.5 At the time the power lapses the nurse of the prescribed class who is responsible for the patient at that time must complete form 16.

Use of restraint

9.6 A nurse invoking section 5(4) is entitled to use the minimum force necessary to prevent the patient from leaving hospital. The general principles that should be applied when the use of restraint has to be considered are set out in paras 19.6 - 19.8.

Management responsibilities

9.7 The use of section 5(4) is an emergency measure and the doctor with the power to use section 5(2) in respect of the patient should treat it as such and arrive as soon as possible. The doctor should not wait six hours before attending simply because this is the maximum time allowed. If the doctor has not arrived within four hours, the duty consultant should be contacted and should attend. Where no doctor has attended within six hours an oral report (suitably recorded) should be made immediately to the responsible senior manager, and a written report should be submitted to that manager and the Hospital Managers on the next working day. The responsible senior manager should nominate a suitable person to supervise the patient's leaving.

9.8 The holding power lapses upon the arrival of the doctor. The six hour holding period counts as part of the 72 hour holding period if the doctor decides to report under section 5(2).

9.9 A suitably qualified, experienced and competent nurse should be on all wards where there is a possibility of section 5(4) being invoked, particularly acute admission wards, and wards where there are acutely disturbed patients, or patients requiring intensive nursing care.

9.10 While it is desirable that a nurse who invokes the power should be qualified in the speciality relevant to the patient's mental disorder the legislation does not require this. Where a nurse may have to apply the power to patients from outside his or her specialist field it is good practice for employers to arrange suitable post-basic education and training, especially in the use of section 5(4). Close working between nurses in different specialities is also important.

The police power to remove to a place of safety (section 136)

(para 317 of the Memorandum)

Good practice

10.1 This depends on:

a. the local Social Services Authority, Health Authority, Trust and the Chief Constable establishing a clear policy for use of the power;

b. all professionals involved in its implementation understanding the power and its purpose, and the person's other rights and following the local policy concerning implementation.

The local policy

10.2 The purpose of removing a person to a place of safety (as defined in section 135(6)) under section 136(2) is to enable him or her to be examined by a doctor and interviewed by an ASW and for any necessary arrangements for his care and treatment to be made. The local policy should ensure that these assessments are conducted effectively and quickly.

10.3 The policy should define the responsibilities of:

a. police officers to remain in attendance where the patient's health or safety or the protection of others so require, when the patient is taken to a place of safety other than a police station;

b. police officers, doctors and ASWs for the satisfactory returning to the community of a person assessed under section 136 who is not admitted to hospital or immediately placed in accommodation.

10.4 The policy should include provisions for the use of the section to be monitored so that:

a. a check can be made of how and in what circumstances it is being used, including its use in relation to ethnic minorities;
b. the parties to the policy can consider any changes in the mental health services that might result in the reduction of its use.

The place of safety

10.5 The identification of preferred places of safety is a matter for local agreement. However, as a general rule it is preferable for a person thought to be suffering from mental disorder to be detained in a hospital rather than a police station. Regard should be had to any impact different types of place of safety may have on the person held and hence on the outcome of an assessment. Once the person has been removed to a particular place of safety, they cannot be transferred to a different place of safety.

Good practice points

10.6 Where an individual is removed to a place of safety by the police under section 136 it is recommended that:

a. where he or she is to be taken to a hospital as a place of safety immediate contact is made by the police with both the hospital and the local social services department;
b. where the police station is to be used as a place of safety immediate contact is made with the local social services authority and the appropriate doctor.

The local policy for the implementation of section 136 should ensure that police officers know whom to contact.

Record keeping

10.7 A record of the person's time of arrival must be made immediately he or she reaches the place of safety. As soon as detention under section 136 ends the individual must be so advised by those who are detaining him or her. The managers of the place of safety should devise and use a form for recording the end of the person's detention under this section (similar to the form used for section 5(4)).

10.8 Section 136 is not an emergency admission section. It enables an individual who falls within its criteria to be detained for the purposes of an assessment by a doctor and ASW, and for any necessary arrangements for his or her treatment and care to be made. When these have been completed within the 72 hour detention period, the authority to detain the patient ceases.

a. Ordinarily, neither a hospital nor the police should discharge an individual detained under section 136 before the end of the 72 hour period without assessments having been made by a doctor and ASW within that period. Where the doctor, having examined the individual, concludes that he or she is not mentally disordered within the meaning of the Act then the individual can no longer be detained under the section and should be immediately discharged from detention.

b. Where a hospital is used as a place of safety it may be better for the patient not to be formally admitted although he or she may have to be cared for on a ward. Where such a policy is adopted it is essential to remember that the patient must be examined by a doctor in the same way as if formally admitted.

c. Where a police station is used as a place of safety speedy assessment is desirable to ensure that the person spends no longer than necessary in police custody but is either returned to the community or admitted to hospital.

Information about rights

10.9 Where an individual has been removed to a place of safety by the police under section 136:

a. the person removed is entitled to have another person, of his or her choice, informed of the removal and his or her whereabouts (section 56 of the Police and Criminal Evidence Act 1984);

b. when the person removed is in police detention (that is, a police station is being used as a place of safety) he or she has a right of access to legal advice (section 58 of the Police and Criminal Evidence Act 1984);

c. where detention is in a place of safety other than a police station access to legal advice should be facilitated whenever it is requested.

It is important to recognise that although the Act uses the term "remove", it is deemed to be an "arrest" for the purposes of the Police and Criminal Evidence Act 1984.

10.10 Where the hospital is used as a place of safety the Hospital Managers must ensure that the provisions of section 132 (giving of information) are complied with.

10.11 Where the police station is a place of safety, although section 132 does not apply, the local policy should require that the same information is given in writing on the person's arrival at the place of safety. There may be scope for co-operation between hospitals and the police in preparing suitable leaflets or letters.

Assessment

10.12 The local implementation policy should ensure that the doctor examining the patient should wherever possible be approved under section 12 of the Act. Where the examination has to be conducted by a doctor who is not approved, the reasons for this should be recorded.

10.13 Assessment by both doctor and social worker should begin as soon as possible after the arrival of the individual at the place of safety. Any implementation policy should set target times for the commencement of the assessment and the Health Authority, Trust and local Social Services Authority should review local practice against these targets.

10.14 The person must be seen by *both* the doctor and the ASW, unless the circumstances set out in para 10.8a apply. The local policy should include the necessary arrangements to enable the person to be jointly assessed.

a. If the doctor sees the person first and concludes that admission to hospital is unnecessary, or the person agrees to informal admission, the individual must still be seen by an ASW, who must consult with the doctor about any other arrangements that might need to be made for his or her treatment and care.

b. It is desirable for a consultant psychiatrist in learning disabilities and an ASW with experience of working with people with learning disabilities to be available to make a joint assessment if it appears that the detained person has a learning disability.

10.15 The role of the ASW includes:

- interviewing the person;
- contacting any relevant relatives/friends;
- ascertaining whether there is a psychiatric history;
- considering any possible alternatives to admission to hospital;
- making arrangements for compulsory admission to hospital;
- making any other necessary arrangements.

Treatment

10.16 Part IV of the Act does not apply to persons detained under section 136. In the absence of consent, the person can only be treated in accordance with the provisions of the common law (see Chapter 15).

Necessary arrangements

10.17 Once the assessment has been concluded it is the responsibility of the doctors and ASW to consider if any necessary arrangements for the person's treatment and care have to be made.

10.18 Where compulsory admission is indicated:

a. where the hospital is the place of safety the person should be admitted either under section 2 or section 3, as appropriate. When the approved doctor providing one recommendation is on the staff of the hospital, the second recommendation should be provided by a doctor with previous knowledge of the person, for example his or her GP. When a person detained under section 136 is not registered with a GP, the second opinion should be provided by a second approved doctor;

b. persons detained under section 136 in hospital pending completion of their assessment should not have their detention extended by use of section 5(2) or section 5(4);

c. where the police station is the place of safety then compulsory admission should be under section 2 or 3 as appropriate. Section 4 may be used if there is an urgent need to move the person to hospital.

Section 135

10.19 Powers of entry under section 135(1) or (2) may be used when it is necessary to gain access to a mentally disordered person who is not in a public place and, if necessary, remove him or her to a place of safety. Local authorities should issue guidance to ASWs on how to use the power.

Conveyance of patients

(Para 31 of the Memorandum)

Powers

11.1 A properly completed application for admission under the Act, together with the required medical recommendations, gives the applicant (ASW or nearest relative) the authority to convey the patient to hospital. In the case of patients subject to after-care under supervision, the supervisor has the power to take and convey the patient to a place where he or she is required to attend for medical treatment, occupation, education or training (see Chapter 28).

General

11.2 Authorities, including the ambulance service and the police, who are involved in conveying patients should agree joint policies and procedures to include:

a. a clear statement of the roles and obligations of each authority and its staff;

b. the form of any authorization to be given by the ASW, or supervisor, to others to convey the patient;

c. guidance on powers in relation to conveying patients.

11.3 The ASW, or supervisor, has a professional obligation to ensure that the most humane and least threatening method of conveying the patient is used, consistent with ensuring that no harm comes to the patient or to others. The ASW or supervisor should take into account:

- the patient's preferences;
- the views of relatives or friends involved with the patient;
- the views of other professionals involved in the application or who know the patient;
- his or her judgment of the patient's state of mind, and the likelihood of the patient behaving in a violent or dangerous manner;
- the impact that any particular mode of conveying the patient will have on the patient's relationship with the community to which he or she will return.

11.4 When conveying a patient to hospital the ASW has the power of a police constable. The task of conveying the patient may be delegated eg. to ambulance staff or the police. The ASW or supervisor retains ultimate responsibly to ensure that the patient is conveyed in a lawful and humane manner and should give guidance to those asked to assist.

11.5 If the patient is conveyed by ambulance, the ASW or supervisor may accompany the patient. Where requested by the applicant, the ambulance authority should make the necessary arrangements. The patient may be accompanied by another person, provided the ASW or supervisor is satisfied that this will not increase the risk of harm to the patient or others.

11.6 The patient should not be conveyed by car unless the ASW or supervisor is satisfied that this would not present danger to the patient or others. There should *always* be an escort for the patient other than the driver.

11.7 If the patient is likely to be violent or dangerous the police should be asked to help. Where possible an ambulance should be used. Otherwise a police vehicle suitable for conveying such a patient should be used. While the police may have to exercise their duty to protect persons or property while the patient is being conveyed they should, where possible, comply with any directions or guidance given by the ASW or supervisor.

Conveying to hospital

11.8 If an ASW is the applicant, he or she has a professional responsibility for ensuring that all the necessary arrangements are made for the patient to be conveyed to hospital.

11.9 If the nearest relative is the applicant, the assistance of an ASW should be made available if requested. If this is not possible, other professionals involved in the admission should give advice and assistance.

11.10 The ASW should telephone the receiving hospital to ensure that the patient is expected and give the likely time of arrival. If possible the ASW should ask the name of the person who will be formally receiving the admission documents.

11.11 The ASW must ensure that the admission documents arrive at the receiving hospital at the same time as the patient. If the ASW is not travelling in the same vehicle as the patient, the documents should be given to the person authorised to convey the patient with instructions for them to be presented to the officer authorised to receive them.

11.12 If the ASW is not travelling with the patient, he or she should arrive at the hospital at the same time or as soon as possible afterwards. He or she should ensure that the admission documents have been delivered, that the admission of the patient is under way and that any relevant information is passed to the hospital staff. The ASW should remain in the hospital with the patient until satisfied that the patient has been detained in a proper manner.

11.13 The ASW should leave an outline report at the hospital when the patient is admitted, giving reasons for the admission and any practical matters about the patient's circumstances which the hospital should know and, where possible, the name and telephone number of a social worker who can give further information. Social services departments should consider the use of a form on which ASWs can make this outline report. A full report should also be prepared for the formal social services department record.

11.14 A patient who has been sedated before being conveyed to hospital should whenever possible be accompanied by a nurse, a doctor or a suitably trained ambulance person experienced in the management of such patients.

11.15 If the ASW or authorised person is refused access to the premises where the patient is, and forcible entry will be needed to remove the patient, an application should be made for a warrant under section 135(2).

Receipt and scrutiny of documents

(Paras 44-54 of the Memorandum)

12.1 The Hospital Managers should formally delegate their duties to receive and scrutinise admission documents to a limited number of officers, with a knowledge of the relevant parts of the Act, who can provide 24 hour cover. A general manager should take overall responsibility on behalf of the Hospital Managers for the proper receipt and scrutiny of documents.

12.2 There is a difference between "receiving" documents and "scrutinising" them. Documents should be scrutinised at the same time as they are received, if possible, otherwise as soon after as possible.

Receipt of documents

12.3

a. If the Hospital Managers' obligation to receive documents is delegated to nursing staff such delegation should be to the nurse in charge of the ward. If the nurse is below the grade of first level nurse, he or she should seek the advice of a first level nurse when "receiving" documents.

b. The hospital should have a checklist for the guidance of those delegated to receive documents, to detect errors which cannot be corrected at a later stage in the procedure (see section 15).

c. When the patient is being admitted on the application of an ASW the person "receiving" the admission documents should check their accuracy with the ASW.

d.   The "receiving" officer should have access to a manager for advice, especially at night.

"Scrutinising documents"

12.4

a.   Where the person delegated to receive the documents is not authorised by the Hospital Managers to rectify a defective admission document, the documents must be scrutinised by a person who is authorised immediately on the patient's admission or during the next working day if admitted at night, during weekends or on public holidays when such a person is not available.

b.   The Hospital Managers must arrange for the medical recommendations to be medically scrutinised, to ensure that they show sufficient legal grounds for detention. The clinical description of the patient's mental condition should include a description of his or her symptoms and behaviour, not merely a diagnostic classification. This scrutiny should be carried out at the same time as the administrative scrutiny.

Hospital Managers

12.5

a.   The Hospital Managers are responsible for ensuring that patients are detained lawfully. They should therefore monitor the receipt and scrutiny of admission documents on a regular basis.

b.   Those delegated to scrutinise documents must be clear about what kind of errors on application forms and medical recommendations can and cannot be corrected *[see paras 46-49 of the Memorandum]*. If no original pink forms are available photocopies of an original form can be used. Current statutory versions of the forms must be used.

c.   Details of defective admission documents, whether rectifiable or not, and of any subsequent action, must be given to the Hospital Managers on a regular basis.

d.   Hospital Managers should ensure that those delegated to receive and scrutinise admission documents understand the requirements of the Act, and if necessary receive appropriate training.

Guardianship (section 7)

(Paras 38-42 of the Memorandum)

Purpose of guardianship

13.1 The purpose of guardianship is to enable patients to receive care in the community where it cannot be provided without the use of compulsory powers. It provides an authoritative framework for working with a patient, with a minimum of constraint, to achieve as independent a life as possible within the community. Where it is used it must be part of the patient's overall care and treatment plan.

13.2 After-care under supervision provides an alternative statutory framework for the after-care of patients who have been detained in hospital for treatment and meet the criteria set out in section 25A of the Act. Detailed guidance on after-care under supervision is given in Chapter 28.

Assessment for guardianship

13.3 ASWs and doctors should consider guardianship as a possible alternative to admission to, or continuing care in, hospital.

13.4 An application for guardianship should be accompanied by a comprehensive care plan established on the basis of multi-disciplinary discussions. It is important that any procedures instituted by social services departments are no more than the minimum necessary to ensure the proper use of guardianship and that guardianship can be used in a positive and flexible manner.

Components of effective guardianship

13.5 A comprehensive care plan is required (under the Care Programme Approach (CPA) in England) which identifies the services needed by the patient and who will provide them. The care plan should include care arrangements, suitable accommodation, treatment and personal support. For those subject to guardianship the care plan should also indicate which of the powers under the Act are necessary to achieve the plan. If no powers are required guardianship should not be used.

13.6 Key elements of the plan should include:

a. depending on the patient's level of "capacity", his or her recognition of the "authority" of, and willingness to work with, the guardian;

b. support from the Local Authority for the guardian;

c. suitable accommodation to help meet the patient's needs;

d. access to day care, education and training facilities;

e. effective co-operation and communication between all persons concerned in implementing the care plan.

The guardian should be willing to 'advocate' on behalf of the patient in relation to those agencies whose services are needed to carry out the care plan.

Duties of Social Services Departments

13.7 Each Local Authority should establish a policy setting out the arrangements for:

a. receiving, considering and scrutinising applications for guardianship. Such arrangements should ensure that applications are properly but speedily dealt with;

b. monitoring the progress of the guardianship including steps to be taken to fulfil the authority's statutory obligations in relation to private guardians and to arrange visits to the patient;

c. ensuring the suitability of any proposed private guardian, and that he or she is able to understand and carry out the statutory duties, including the appointment of a nominated medical attendant;

d. ensuring that patients under guardianship receive, both orally and in writing, relevant aspects of the information that Hospital Managers are required to give to detained patients under section 132 (patient leaflets 10 and 11);

e. ensuring that the patient is aware of his or her right to apply to a Mental Health Review Tribunal and that a named officer of the local authority will give any necessary assistance to the patient in making such an application;

f. maintaining detailed records relating to the person under guardianship;

g. ensuring the review of the guardianship towards the end of each period of guardianship;

h. discharging the patient from guardianship as soon as it is no longer required.

The powers of the guardian

13.8 Section 8 of the Act sets out the three powers of the guardian as follows:

a. to require the patient to live at a place specified by the guardian. This does not provide the legal authority to detain a patient physically or remove the patient against his or her wishes. A patient who is absent without leave from the specified place may be returned within the statutory time limit *[see paras 72-74 of the Memorandum]* by those authorised to do so under the Act;

b. to require the patient to attend at specified places for medical treatment, occupation, education or training. If the patient refuses to attend, the guardian is not authorised to use force to secure such attendance, nor does the Act enable medical treatment to be administered in the absence of the patient's consent;

c. to require access to the patient to be given at the place where he or she is living to persons detailed in the Act. A refusal without reasonable cause to permit an authorised person to have access to the patient is an offence under section 129 but no force may be used to secure entry.

If the patient consistently resists the exercise of the guardian's powers it can be concluded that guardianship is not the most appropriate form of care for that person and the guardianship order should be discharged.

13.9 Points to remember:

a. Guardianship does not restrict the patient's access to hospital services on an informal basis. A patient who requires treatment but does not need to be detained may be admitted informally.

b. Guardianship can also remain in force if the patient is admitted to hospital under section 2 or 4 but not under section 3.

c. It is possible in certain circumstances for a patient liable to be detained in hospital by virtue of an application under Part II of the Act to be transferred into guardianship and for a person subject to guardianship under Part II of the Act to be transferred into the guardianship of another local social services authority or person approved by such authority or to be transferred to hospital. (See section 19 and regulations 7-9 of the Mental Health (Hospital, Guardianship and Consent to Treatment) Regulations 1983).

13.10 Particular practice issues:

a. Guardianship must not be used to require a patient to reside in hospital except where it is necessary for a very short time in order to provide shelter whilst accommodation in the community is being arranged.

b. Where an adult is assessed as requiring residential care, but owing to mental incapacity is unable to make a decision as to whether he or she wishes to be placed in residential care, those who are responsible for his or her care should consider the applicability and appropriateness of guardianship for providing the framework within which decisions about his or her current and future care can be planned.

Guardianship under section 37

13.11 Guardianship may be used as an alternative to hospital orders by courts where the prescribed criteria, which are similar to those of a hospital order, are met. The court should be satisfied that the Local Authority or named person is willing to act as guardian. The Local Authority should be satisfied with the arrangements. In considering the appropriateness of guardianship they should be guided by the same principles as apply under Part II of the Act. The powers and duties conferred on the local authority or private guardian and the provisions as to duration, renewal and discharge are the same as in guardianship applications except that the power to discharge is not available to the nearest relative.

Information for detained patients, those subject to guardianship and nearest relatives

(Paras 297-302 of the Memorandum)

14.1 Under section 132 the Hospital Managers must ensure that all detained patients are given and understand:

a. specific information as soon as is practicable after their admission *[see section 132 and para 297 of the Memorandum]*;

b. particular information in so far as it is relevant to the patient *[see section 132(2) and para 298 of the Memorandum]*.

14.2 The managers are also required to ensure that the above information is given in writing to the patient's nearest relative - unless the patient wishes otherwise. Health Authorities and Trusts are reminded that sample letters to nearest relatives were circulated at Annex B of Circular HC(83)17.

14.3 Under Section 133 the Hospital Managers should, if the patient does not object, give the nearest relative of a detained patient at least seven days notice of his or her discharge from detention in a hospital or mental nursing home (unless the nearest relative requests not to be kept informed). It is good practice, if the patient agrees, for the nearest relative to be provided with details of any care the patient will be receiving once discharged from detention in hospital.

The Hospital Managers' information policy

14.4 In order to fulfil their statutory duties Hospital Managers should implement a system which is consistent with the principles set out in Chapter 1 and ensures that:

a. the correct information is given to the patient;

b. the information is given in a suitable manner and at a suitable time and in accordance with the requirements of the law;

c. the member of staff who is to give the information has received sufficient training and guidance and is identified in relation to each detained patient;

d. a record is kept of the information given, including how, when, where and by whom it was given;

e. a regular check is made that information has been properly given to each detained patient, and understood by them.

Specific information

14.5

a. *Information on consent to treatment*

The patient must be informed;

- of the nature, purpose and likely effects of the treatment which is planned;

- of their rights to withdraw their consent to treatment at any time and of the need for consent to be given to any further treatment;

- how and when treatment can be given without their consent, including by the second opinion process and when treatment has begun if stopping it would cause serious suffering to the patient.

b. *Information on detention, renewal and discharge*

The patient should be informed:

- of the provisions of the Act under which they are detained, and the reasons for their detention;

- that they will not automatically be discharged when the current period of detention ends;
- that their detention will not automatically be renewed when the current period of detention ends;
- of their right to have their views about their continued detention or discharge considered before any decision is made.

c. *Information on applications to Mental Health Review Tribunals*

Patients and nearest relatives must be informed:

- of their rights to apply to Mental Health Review Tribunals;
- about the role of the Tribunal;
- how to apply to a Tribunal;
- how to contact a suitably qualified solicitor;
- that free Legal Aid - Advice By Way Of Representation (ABWOR) may be available;
- how to contact any other organisation which may be able to help them make an application to a Tribunal.

d. *Information on the Mental Health Act Commission*

Patients must be informed:

- about the role of the Mental Health Act Commission;
- when the Commission is to visit a hospital or unit;
- of their right to meet the Commissioners;
- of their right to complain to the Commission.

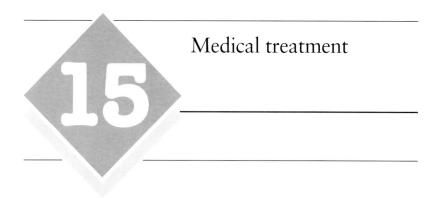

Medical treatment

(Paras 212-230 of the Memorandum)

Introduction

15.1 This chapter gives guidance on medical treatment, capacity (see paras 15.9 -15.12), consent to treatment (see paras 15.13-15.17) and the treatment of those without capacity (see paras 15.18-15.24).

Duty of rmo

15.2 Everyone involved in the medical treatment of mental disorder should be familiar with the provisions of Part IV of the Act, related statutory instruments, relevant circulars and advice notes. But it is for the rmo to ensure that there is compliance with the Act's provisions relating to medical treatment.

Duty of the Hospital Managers

15.3 The managers should monitor compliance with the provisions of Part IV of the Act. (For a more detailed discussion of Part IV of the Act see Chapter 16).

Medical treatment

15.4 For the purposes of the Act, medical treatment includes nursing and care, habilitation and rehabilitation under medical supervision, ie the broad range of activities aimed at alleviating, or preventing a deterioration of, the patient's mental disorder. It includes physical treatment such as ECT and the administration of drugs, and psychotherapy.

Treatment plans

15.5 Treatment plans are essential for both informal and detained patients. Consultants should co-ordinate the formulation of a treatment plan in consultation with their professional colleagues. The plan should form part of a coherent care plan under the CPA, for patients in England, and be recorded in the patient's clinical notes.

15.6 A treatment plan should include a description of the immediate and long term goals for the patient with a clear indication of the treatments proposed and the methods of treatment. The patient's progress and possible changes to the care programme should be reviewed at regular intervals.

15.7 Wherever possible the whole care programme should be discussed with the patient, with a view to enabling him or her to contribute to it and express agreement or disagreement. The care programme should be discussed with the patient's relatives or carers, with the consent of the patient if he or she is capable of giving consent, and, if the patient is not capable, on the basis of whatever discussions are necessary in the best interests of the patient.

Capacity and consent to treatment: introduction

15.8 Under the common law, valid consent (see para 15.13) is required from all patients before medical treatment can be given, except where common law or statute provides authority to give treatment without consent. The common law may authorise treatment where the patient is incapable of consenting or, rarely, where the patient may be capable of consent. Treatment may be authorised by statute for example under Part IV of the Act (see Chapter 16).

Capacity to make treatment decisions

15.9 The assessment of a patient's capacity to make a decision about his or her own medical treatment is a matter for clinical judgment, guided by current professional practice and subject to legal requirements. It is the personal responsibility of any doctor proposing to treat a patient to determine whether the patient has capacity to give a valid consent.

Capacity: the basic principles

15.10 An individual is presumed to have the capacity to make a treatment decision unless he or she:

- is unable to take in and retain the information material to the decision especially as to the likely consequences of having or not having the treatment; or
- is unable to believe the information; or
- is unable to weigh the information in the balance as part of a process of arriving at the decision[5, 6]

It must be remembered that:

- any assessment as to an individual's capacity has to be made in relation to a particular treatment or admission proposal;
- capacity in an individual with a mental disorder can be variable over time and should be assessed at the time the admission or treatment is proposed;
- all assessments of an individual's capacity should be fully recorded in the patient's medical notes.

15.11 Where an individual lacks capacity at a particular time it may be possible to establish that there was an advance refusal of treatment in the past. To be valid an advance refusal must be clearly verifiable and must relate to the type of treatment now proposed. If there is any reason to doubt the reliability of an advance refusal of treatment, then an application to the court for a declaration could be made[7]. The individual must have had the capacity to make an advance refusal when it was made. An advance refusal of medical treatment for mental disorder does not prevent the authorization of such treatment by Part IV of the Act in the circumstances where those provisions apply.

15.12 Mental disorder does not necessarily make a patient incapable of giving or refusing consent. Capacity to consent is variable in people with

---

[5] Re C (Refusal of Treatment) [1994] 1 FLR 31
[6] Re MB [1997] 2 FCR 541
[7] see Guideline 3 in R v Collins ex parte S (No. 2) [1998]

mental disorder and should be assessed in relation to the particular patient, at the particular time, as regards the particular treatment proposed. Not everyone is equally capable of understanding the same explanation of a treatment plan. The explanation should be appropriate to the level of his or her assessed ability.

Consent: the basic principles

15.13 'Consent' is the voluntary and continuing permission of the patient to receive a particular treatment, based on an adequate knowledge of the purpose, nature, likely effects and risks of that treatment including the likelihood of its success and any alternatives to it. Permission given under any unfair or undue pressure is not 'consent'.

Consent from patients with capacity to consent

15.14 It is the duty of everyone proposing to give treatment to use reasonable care and skill, not only in giving information prior to seeking a patient's consent but also in meeting the continuing obligation to provide the patient with adequate information about the proposed treatment and alternatives to it.

15.15 The information which must be given should be related to the particular patient, the particular treatment and the relevant medical knowledge and practice. In every case sufficient information must be given to ensure that the patient understands in broad terms the nature, likely effects and risks of that treatment including the likelihood of its success and any alternatives to it. Additional information is a matter of professional judgment for the doctor proposing the treatment.

15.16 The patient should be invited to ask questions and the doctor should answer fully, frankly and truthfully. There may be a compelling reason, in the patient's interests, for not disclosing certain information. A doctor who chooses not to disclose must be prepared to justify the decision. If a doctor chooses not to answer a patient's question, he or she should make this clear to the patient so that the patient knows where he or she stands.

15.17 The patient should be told that his or her consent to treatment can be withdrawn at any time and that fresh consent is required before further treatment can be given or reinstated. The patient should receive an explanation of the likely consequences of not receiving the treatment. (See para 16.11 on withdrawing consent in relation to treatment administered under Part IV of the Act.)

Treatment of those without capacity to consent

15.18 The administration of medical treatment to people incapable of taking their own treatment decisions is a matter of much concern to professionals and others involved in their care. It is the personal responsibility of professionals to ensure that they understand the relevant law.

15.19 Principles governing a child's capacity to consent to treatment are set out in Chapter 31.

15.20 An adult patient may be mentally incapable of consenting to treatment or refusing treatment (see paras 15.9-15.12). The mental incapacity may be due to temporary factors such as delirium, shock, pain or drugs, or mental incapacity may be more long-lasting as with patients who have severe learning disabilities or some patients who suffer from a degenerative condition such as Alzheimer's disease.

15.21 There are particular considerations that doctors must take into account in discharging their duty of care for those who lack capacity to consent. Treatment for their condition may be prescribed for them in their best interests under the common law doctrine of necessity[8]. According to the decision in the case of in Re F, if treatment is given to a patient who is not capable of giving consent "in the patient's best interests", the treatment must be:

- necessary to save life or prevent a deterioration or ensure an improvement in the patient's physical or mental health; and
- in accordance with a practice accepted at the time by a reasonable body of medical opinion skilled in the particular form of treatment in question[9].

---

[8] see the decisions in the House of Lords in Re F [1990] 2 AC 1 and R v Bournewood Community and Mental Health NHS Trust ex parte L [1998] 3 ALL ER 289

[9] The test that was originally laid down in Bolam v Friern Hospital Management Committee [1957] 1 WLR 582.

15.22 There are exceptional circumstances in which the proposed treatment should not be carried out on mentally incapacitated patients without first seeking the approval of the High Court by way of a declaration. Sterilisation, according to the House of Lords in Re F, is one such circumstance.

15.23 The procedures to be used when applying for a declaration that a proposed operation for sterilisation is lawful were set out initially by Lord Brandon of Oakbrook in Re F and developed by the Official Solicitor[10]. In outline, the procedure is as follows:

a. applications for a declaration that a proposed operation for sterilisation of a patient can lawfully be carried out despite the inability of such patient to consent thereto should be by way of Originating Summons issuing out of the Family Division of the High Court;

b. the applicant should normally be the person(s) responsible for the care of the patient or intending to carry out the proposed operation or other treatment, if it is declared to be lawful;

c. the patient must always be a party and should normally be a respondent. In cases in which the patient is a respondent the patient's guardian ad litem should normally be the Official Solicitor. In any cases in which the Official Solicitor is not either the 'next friend' or the guardian ad litem of the patient or an applicant he shall be respondent;

d. with a view to protecting the patient's privacy, but subject always to the judge's discretion, the hearing will be in chambers, but the decision and the reasons for that decision will be given in court.

15.24 *The Handbook of Contraceptive Practice* (*Department of Health 1990*) considers the effect of Re F on operations for sterilisation, as well as other matters relating to the sexuality of people with learning disabilities.

---

[10] Practice Note (Official Solicitor: Sterilisation) [1996] 2 FLR 111.

Treatment of those who may have capacity to consent where consent is not given

15.25 A patient capable of giving consent can only be given medical treatment for mental disorder against his or her wishes in accordance with the provisions of Part IV of the Act. In an emergency, where it is not possible immediately to apply the provisions of the Mental Health Act, a patient suffering from a mental disorder which is leading to behaviour that is an immediate serious danger to him or herself or to other people may be given such treatment as represents the minimum necessary response to avert that danger. The administration of such treatment is not an alternative to giving treatment under the Mental Health Act and its administration should not delay the proper application of the Act to the patient at the earliest opportunity (see Chapter 16).

Medical treatment and second opinions

16

(Paras 212-230 of the Memorandum)

General

16.1 The common law (see Chapter 15) applies to patients detained under the Act but additional provisions affecting medical treatment of detained patients are to be found in Part IV of the Act. Part IV of the Act provides specific statutory authority for forms of medical treatment for mental disorder to be given to most patients liable to be detained, without their consent in certain circumstances. It also provides specific safeguards. Patients 'liable to be detained' are those who are detained or have been granted leave of absence (section 17). Part IV also provides specific safeguards to all patients (whether detained or not) in relation to treatments that give rise to special concern.

16.2 The provisions of Part IV can be summarized as follows:

a. **Section 57 - Treatments requiring the patient's consent and a second opinion** - psychosurgery and the surgical implantation of hormones for the reduction of male sexual drive. These provisions apply to all patients whether or not they are liable to be detained.

b. **Section 58 - Treatments requiring the patient's consent or a second opinion** - the administration of medicine beyond three months and treatment by ECT at any time. These provisions apply to all patients liable to be detained except those detained under section 4, sections 5(2) or 5(4), sections 35, 135, 136 and 37(4); also patients conditionally discharged under section 42(2) and sections 73 and 74. Patients subject to those sections can be treated under common law.

c. **Section 62 - Urgent Treatment** - in certain circumstances the safeguards in sections 57 and 58 do not apply where urgent treatment is required (see para 16.40-16.41). Section 62 is only applicable to those patients and types of treatments set out in a and b above.

d. **Section 63 - Treatments that do not require the patient's consent** - all medical treatments for mental disorder given by or under the direction of the patient's rmo and which are not referred to in sections 57 or 58. This provision applies to the same patients as section 58.

16.3 Everyone involved in the operation of Part IV of the Act should be familiar with:

a. the provisions of Part IV of the Act;

b. *paras 212-230 of the Memorandum*;

c. DHSS circular Dear Doctor Letter (DDL) (84)4.

In addition, rmos should obtain copies of 'Advice to Second Opinion Appointed Doctors' published by the Mental Health Act Commission.

16.4 A detained patient is not necessarily incapable of giving consent. The patient's consent should be sought for all proposed treatments which may lawfully be given under the Act. It is the personal responsibility of the patient's current rmo to ensure that valid consent has been sought. The interview at which such consent was sought should be properly recorded in the medical notes.

16.5 Part IV of the Act applies to medical treatment for mental disorder. Medical treatment may be interpreted as including care and treatment to alleviate the symptoms of mental disorder[11]. Part IV does not apply to the treatment of physical disorders unless it can reasonably be said that the physical disorder is a symptom or underlying cause of the mental disorder. If in doubt the rmo should seek legal advice. (See also the Mental Health Act Commission's Guidance Note 3 on Anorexia Nervosa).

Section 57 - Treatments requiring consent and a second opinion

16.6 A decision to give treatment under section 57 requires careful con-

---

[11] B v Croydon Health Authority [1995] 2 WLR 294

sideration because of the ethical issues and possible long-term effects. Procedures for implementing this section must be agreed between the Mental Health Act Commission and the hospitals concerned.

16.7 Before the rmo or doctor in charge of treatment refers the case to the Mental Health Act Commission:

a. the referring doctor should personally satisfy him or herself that the patient is capable of giving valid consent and has consented;

b. the patient and, if the patient agrees, his or her close relatives and carers should be told that the patient's willingness to undergo treatment does not necessarily mean that the treatment will be given. The patient should be made fully aware of the provisions of section 57;

c. for psychosurgery, the consultant considering the patient's case should have fully assessed the patient as suitable for psychosurgery;

d. for psychosurgery, the case should be referred to the Commission before the patient is transferred to the neuro-surgical centre for the operation. The Commission organises the attendance of two appointed persons and a doctor. The appointed persons and the doctor will usually visit and interview the patient at the referring hospital at an early stage in the procedure;

e. for surgical implantation of hormones for the purpose of reducing male sexual drive, the relationship of the sexual disorder to mental disorder, the nature of treatment, the likely effects and benefits of treatment and knowledge about possible long-term effects require considerable care and caution should be observed.

16.8 Section 57 refers to the surgical implantation of hormones only for the reduction of male sexual drive where it is administered as a medical treatment for mental disorder. If there is any doubt as to whether it is a mental disorder which is being treated, independent legal and medical advice must be sought. The advice of the Mental Health Act Commission should also be obtained about arrangements for implementing section 57 where necessary.

Section 58 - Treatments requiring consent or a second opinion: ECT

16.9 When ECT is proposed valid consent should always be sought by the patient's rmo:

a. if the patient consents the rmo or the Second Opinion Appointed Doctor (SOAD) should complete form 38 and include on the form the proposed maximum number of applications of ECT. In addition, a record of the discussion with the patient with reference to his or her capacity to consent should be made by the rmo in the medical notes. Such information should be included in the patient's treatment plan;

b. if:

- the patient withdraws consent which has been given, or

- there is a break in the continuity of the patient's detention, or

- there is a change in the rmo,

the form 38 lapses and consent should be given again on a fresh form 38 or a second opinion obtained. Arrangements should be made for ensuring that invalid consent forms are clearly marked as lapsed;

c. if the patient's valid consent is not forthcoming, or is withdrawn, or if his or her wishes appear to fluctuate and the rmo plans to proceed with the treatment, the rmo must comply with the requirements of section 58, which should be initiated as soon as possible (see paras 16.20-16.34).

16.10 Patients treated with ECT should be given a leaflet which helps them to understand and remember, both during and after the course of ECT, the advice given about its nature, purpose and likely effects.

Section 58 - Treatments requiring consent or a second opinion: Medication

a. The first three months

16.11 The 3 month period gives time for the doctor to develop a treatment programme suitable for the patient's needs. Even though the Act allows treatment to be given without consent during the first three months the rmo should ensure that the patient's valid consent is sought before any medication is administered. The patient's consent or refusal should be recorded in the case notes. If such consent is not forthcoming or is withdrawn during this period, the rmo must consider whether to proceed in the absence of consent, to give alternative treatment or no further treatment.

16.12 The 3 month period starts on the occasion when medication for mental disorder was first administered by any means during a period of continuing detention. This does not include detention under sections 5(2) or 5(4) (holding power), section 35 (remand to hospital), section 37(4) (court order for detention in a place of safety), section 135 (warrant for removal to a place of safety), and section 136 (removal to a place of safety). The medication does not necessarily have to be administered continuously throughout the three months. The definition of this period is not affected by renewal of the patient's detention, withdrawal of consent, leave of absence or change in or discontinuance of the treatment. A fresh period will only begin if there is a break in the patient's liability for detention. Detention should never be allowed to expire as a means of enabling a fresh three month period to start.

b.   Medication after three months

16.13 A system should be in place for reminding both rmos and patients at least four weeks before the expiry of the three months. Before the three month period ends the patient's current rmo should personally seek his or her consent to any continuing medication, and such consent should be sought for any subsequent administration of medication. A record of the discussion with the patient with reference to his or her capacity to consent should be made by the rmo in the medical notes.

16.14 If the patient consents, the rmo must certify accordingly (form 38). On the certificate the rmo should indicate all drugs proposed, including medication given "as required", either by name or, ensuring that the number of drugs authorised in each class is indicated, by the classes described in the British National Formulary (BNF). The maximum dosage and route of administration should be clearly indicated for each drug or category of drugs proposed.

16.15 Specific advice relating to the inclusion of clozapine in a treatment programme is given in the Mental Health Act Commission's Practice Note 1 (June 1993).

16.16 The original form 38 should be kept with the original detention papers, and copies kept in the case notes and with the patient's medicine chart, so as to ensure that the patient is given only medication to which he or she has consented. It is important that all such additional copies are cancelled if the patient's consent is withdrawn (see para 16.19 below). If the patient's consent is not forthcoming the rmo must comply with the safeguard requirements of section 58. For urgent treatment section 62 may apply (see paras 16.40-16.41).

16.17 The rmo should satisfy him or herself that consent remains valid. It is advisable to seek a second opinion under the section 58 procedures if there is doubt about whether the patient is consenting or not, or if his or her wishes appear to fluctuate.

c.   Nurses and the administration of medication

16.18 Advice on the position of nurses in relation to the administration of medication is given in the Mental Health Act Commission's Practice Note 2 (March 1994)

Withdrawal of consent

16.19 A patient being treated in accordance with section 58 may withdraw consent at any time. Fresh consent or the implementing of section 58 procedures is then required before further treatment can be carried out or reinstated. Where the patient withdraws consent he or she should receive a clear explanation, which should be recorded in the patient's records:

•   of the likely consequences of not receiving the treatment;

•   that a second medical opinion under Part IV of the Act may or will be sought, if applicable, in order to authorise treatment in the continuing absence of the patient's consent;

- of the doctor's power to begin or continue urgent treatment under section 62 until a second medical opinion has been obtained, if applicable.

All consent forms which have become invalid because the patient has withdrawn consent must be clearly marked as cancelled.

Procedure for second opinions

a. *The Role of the Second Opinion Appointed Doctor (SOAD) [see paras 216-221 of the Memorandum]*

16.20 The role of the SOAD is to provide an additional safeguard to protect the patient's rights. When interviewing a patient the SOAD must determine whether he or she is capable of giving valid consent. If the patient does not give or is not capable of giving consent, the SOAD has to determine whether the treatment proposed by the rmo is likely to alleviate or prevent a deterioration of the patient's condition and should be given.

16.21 The SOAD acts as an individual and must reach his or her own judgment as to whether the proposed treatment is reasonable in the light of the general consensus of appropriate treatment for such a condition. In reaching this judgment the SOAD should consider not only the therapeutic efficacy of the proposed treatment but also, where a capable patient is withholding consent, the reasons for such withholding, which should be given their due weight.

16.22 The SOAD should seek professional opinion about the nature of the patient's disorder and problems, the appropriateness of various forms of treatment including that proposed, and the patient's likely response to different types of treatment. The SOAD should take into account any previous experience of comparable treatment of a similar episode of disorder. The SOAD should give due weight to the opinion, knowledge, experience and skill of those consulted.

b. *Responsibilities of the Hospital Managers*

16.23 In anticipation of, and preparation for, a consultation under Part IV, the Hospital Managers and their staff should ensure that:

a. the statutory documents are in order and available to the SOAD;

b. a system exists for reminding the rmo prior to the expiry of the limit set by section 58 and section 61 and for checking the doctor's response;

c. a system exists for letting the patient know towards the expiry of the '3 month period' that his or her consent, or a second opinion, is required;

d. appropriate personnel, including a person other than a doctor or nurse professionally concerned with the patient's care are available (see para 16.31b).

c. *Arranging and preparing for the visit of the SOAD*

16.24 If a SOAD visit is required, the patient's rmo has the personal responsibility of ensuring that the request is made. He or she should ensure that the arrangements are made with the Mental Health Act Commission. Ordinarily, the Commission aims to arrange for a visit from a SOAD to take place within two working days of the request where ECT is proposed, and, in the case of medication, five working days.

16.25 The treatment proposal for the patient, together with notes of any relevant multidisciplinary discussion, must be given to the SOAD before or at the time of the visit. The Hospital Managers, in consultation with the rmo, are responsible for ensuring that the patient is available to meet the SOAD and that the following people are available in person at the time the SOAD visits:

- the patient's rmo;
- the statutory 'consultees' (see para 16.31);
- any other relevant persons;

and that the following documents are available:

- the patient's original detention documents wherever possible or copies of such documents. The original document should be available for viewing by the SOAD if he or she requests;
- all the patient's case notes including records of past responses to similar treatment.

It is desirable that a single professional record is kept for each patient which contains all records relating to that patient. Adequate facilities must be made available for the visit.

d.   The visit of the SOAD

16.26 During a visit the SOAD should:

a.   in the case of a treatment under section 58, satisfy him or herself that the patient's detention papers are in order;

b.   interview the patient in private if possible. Others may attend if the patient and the SOAD agree, or if it is thought that the doctor would be at significant risk of physical harm from the patient;

c.   discuss the case with the patient's rmo face to face, or on the telephone in exceptional circumstances;

d.   consult with two other persons professionally concerned with the patient's care as statutorily required (ie the 'statutory consultees'). The SOAD should be prepared, where appropriate, to consult a wider range of persons professionally concerned with the patient's care than those required by the Act and, with the patient's consent, the patient's nearest relative, family, carers or advocates.

16.27 The SOAD may not be able to reach a decision at the time of the first visit. In these circumstances the patient should be told of the delay. Once a decision has been reached, it is the rmo's responsibility to inform the patient of the SOAD's decision. Only when the SOAD has signed form 39 may treatment be given without the patient's consent, except as provided in section 62. The SOAD may direct that a review report on the treatment be sent to the Mental Health Act Commission at a date earlier than the next date for review under section 61.

16.28 Every attempt should be made by the rmo and the SOAD to reach agreement. If the SOAD is unable to agree with the rmo, the rmo should be informed by the SOAD personally as soon as possible. It is good practice for the SOAD to give reasons for his or her dissent. Neither doctor should allow a disagreement in any way to prejudice the interests of the patient. If agreement cannot be reached, the position should be recorded in the patient's case notes by the rmo who will continue to have responsibility for the patient's management.

16.29 The opinion given by the SOAD is the latter's personal responsibility. It cannot be appealed against to the Mental Health Act Commission.

16.30 If the patient's situation subsequently changes the rmo may contact the Mental Health Act Commission and request a further second opinion. In these circumstances it is the policy of the Commission to ask the same SOAD to return.

e.   Role of the 'statutory consultees.'

16.31 The SOAD must consult:

a.   a nurse, who must be qualified (nursing assistants, auxiliaries and aides are excluded) and has been professionally concerned with the patient's care;

b.   another person similarly concerned, who has direct knowledge of the patient in their professional capacity, and who is neither a nurse nor a doctor; for example, a social worker, occupational therapist, psychologist, psychotherapist, or pharmacist.

16.32 Any person whom the SOAD proposes to consult must consider whether he or she is sufficiently concerned professionally with the patient's care to fulfil the function. If not, or if the person feels that someone else is better placed to fulfil the function, he or she should make this known to the patient's rmo and the SOAD in good time.

16.33 Both consultees may expect a private discussion (only in exceptional cases on the telephone) with the SOAD and to be listened to with consideration.

16.34 Amongst the issues that the 'consultees' should consider commenting upon are:

•   the proposed treatment and the patient's ability to consent to it;

- other treatment options;
- the way in which the decision to treat was arrived at;
- the facts of the case, progress, attitude of relatives etc;
- the implications of imposing treatment upon a non-consenting patient and the reasons for the patient's refusal of treatment;
- any other matter relating to the patient's care on which the 'consultee' wishes to comment.

'Consultees' should ensure that they make a record of their consultation with the SOAD which is placed in the patient's records.

Review of treatment

a. General

16.35 All treatments, whether or not section 61 applies to them, should be regularly reviewed and the patient's treatment plan should include details of when this will take place. Where a patient is receiving treatment under section 58(3)(a), ie. the patient has consented and form 38 has been completed, the form 38 should always have been completed by either the patient's rmo or the SOAD. Although the Act does not direct review of the validity of form 38, it is good practice for them to be reviewed at regular intervals. When such a review is carried out and it is found that the conditions are satisfied a new form 38 should be completed, if appropriate. A new form should also be completed:

- if there is a change in the treatment plan from that recorded;
- if consent is re-established after being withdrawn;
- when there is a break in the patient's detention;
- when there is a permanent change of rmo;
- when the patient's detention is renewed (or annually, whichever is earlier);
- if there is a change in the hospital where the patient is detained.

If the patient no longer consents and it is considered that the treatment should still be given, a second opinion must be sought.

b. Section 61

16.36 When a patient has been treated under section 57 or section 58, when a SOAD has authorised treatment in the absence of the patient's consent, a review by the Mental Health Act Commission on behalf of the Secretary of State has to take place:

a. in the circumstances set out in section 61 (all professionals involved should be familiar with the procedures for completing form MHAC1);

b. where the SOAD has time limited his or her certificate or made it conditional on the making of a review report on the treatment at a date earlier than the first statutory review (See MHAC1).

Once the treatment has been reviewed and form MHAC1 completed, a copy of that form should be given to the patient.

16.37 When submitting a report under section 61, the rmo should advise the Mental Health Act Commission if a patient for whom a certificate of second opinion has previously been issued has since given consent and the consent is still valid. After receipt of a review report, the Mental Health Act Commission will, when necessary, send a SOAD to reassess the patient and decide whether the treatment should continue.

Section 63 treatments not requiring the patient's consent

16.38 Apart from the forms of treatment specified in sections 57 and 58, treatment for the patient's mental disorder which is given by or under the direction of the rmo does not require the patient's consent - although consent should always be sought. As well as medication in the first three months (see paras 16.11-16.12) section 63 covers a wide range of thera-peutic activities involving a variety of professional staff and includes in particular psychological and social therapies. Medical treatment is de-fined in section 145 (see para 16.5 for a reference to relevant case law).

16.39 In practice, it is unlikely that these psychological and social thera-pies could be undertaken without the patient's acceptance and active co-operation. Acceptance in relation to such procedures requires a clear expression of agreement between the patient and the therapist before the treatment has begun. The agreement should be expressed positively in terms of willingness to co-operate rather than as an indication of passive submission (see also paras 18.1 - 18.10).

Urgent treatment

16.40 Any decision to treat a patient urgently under section 62 is a responsibility of the patient's rmo or, in the rmo's absence, of the doctor for the time being in charge of his or her treatment. The rmo, or other doctor, should bear in mind the following considerations:

a. Treatment can only be given where it is immediately necessary to achieve one of the objects set out in section 62 and it is not possible to comply with the safeguards of Part IV of the Act. It is insufficient for the proposed treatment to be simply 'necessary' or 'beneficial.'

b. The section specifically limits the use of 'irreversible' or 'hazardous' treatments. The patient's rmo, or other doctor, is responsible for judging whether treatment falls into either of these categories, and whether therefore the Act allows it to be given, having regard to generally accepted medical opinion.

c. Urgent treatment given under section 62 can only continue for as long as it is immediately necessary to achieve the statutory objective(s).

d. Before deciding to give treatment under section 62 the patient's rmo, or the doctor for the time being in charge of his or her treatment, should wherever possible discuss the proposed urgent treatment with others involved with the patient's care.

It is essential that rmos, or the doctor for the time being in charge of the patient's treatment, have a clear understanding of the circumstances when section 62 applies (see para 16.2.c).

16.41 The Hospital Managers should monitor the use of section 62 in their hospitals. They should ensure that a form is devised to be completed by the patient's rmo or the doctor for the time being in charge of the patient's treatment, every time urgent treatment is given under section 62, giving details of:

- the proposed treatment;
- why it is of urgent necessity to give the treatment;
- the length of time for which the treatment was given.

Responsibilities for operating Part IV

16.42 Promoting the welfare of the patient by the implementation of Part IV and its safeguards requires careful planning and management. The patient's rmo is personally responsible for ensuring that Part IV procedures are followed in relation to that patient. Such responsibility is a continuing one and will apply even if a doctor other than the rmo acts under section 62.

16.43 Overall responsibility for ensuring that the provisions of the Act are complied with rests with the Hospital Managers who should ensure that proper arrangements are made to enable rmos to discharge their responsibilities, but all professional staff involved with the implementation of Part IV should be familiar with its provisions and the procedures for its implementation in the hospital.

16.44 Patients have a statutory right to be informed about the provisions of Part IV of the Act as it relates to them. They should be reminded by letter in addition to receiving the statutory leaflet when either their consent to treatment is needed or a second opinion is due.

Part III of the Act - patients concerned with criminal proceedings

Treatment and care in hospital

17.1 A patient who is remanded to hospital for a report (section 35) or for treatment (section 36) is entitled to obtain, at his or her own expense, or through Legal Aid, an independent report on his or her mental condition from a registered medical practitioner of the patient's choosing for the purpose of applying to court for the termination of the remand. The Hospital Managers should help in the exercise of this right by enabling the patient to contact a suitably qualified and experienced solicitor, or other adviser.

17.2 The consent to treatment provisions of the Act do not apply to patients remanded under section 35, so in the absence of the patient's consent, treatment can only be administered in an emergency under the provisions of the common law (see Chapter 15).

17.3 Where a patient remanded under section 35 is thought to be in need of medical treatment for mental disorder under Part IV of the Act, the patient should be referred back to court as soon as possible with an appropriate recommendation, and with an assessment of whether he or she is in a fit state to attend court. If there is a delay in securing a court date, consideration should be given to whether the patient meets the criteria for detention under section 3 of the Act.

17.4 A report prepared in pursuit of a section 35 remand order should contain:

- a statement as to whether a patient is suffering from a specified form of mental disorder as required by the section, identifying its relevance to the alleged offence. The report should not comment on guilt or innocence. It may be appropriate to suggest that a further report be submitted to the court between conviction and sentence;

- relevant social factors;

- any recommendations on care and treatment, including where and when it should take place and who should be responsible.

Psychological treatments

18.1 Psychological treatments carried out competently can be beneficial to patients. If carried out incompetently they can be harmful. Some treatments interfere with patients' basic human rights and it is important that no one deprives a patient of food, shelter, water, warmth, a comfortable environment, confidentiality or reasonable privacy (both physical and in relation to their personal feelings and thoughts). The possibility of misapplication of techniques and serious errors in therapy can be reduced by ensuring that people offering such treatments (on an individual or group basis) are appropriately qualified and supervised, and that they demonstrate a commitment to evidence-based practice. Recruitment and selection procedures should ensure appropriate qualification, using appropriate external assessors. A medical or nursing qualification does not, in itself, confer competence to practise psychotherapeutic treatment. Membership of, or affiliation to, an appropriate professional body may help to promote the maintenance of a high standard of professional practice.

18.2 The Hospital Managers must ensure that psychological treatment programmes are set out clearly so that they can be understood by staff, patients and relatives. Guidelines should include procedures for noting and monitoring their use. A person with sufficient skills in implementing programmes should be available to monitor procedures as well as the progress of patients.

18.3 Any programme of psychological treatment should form part of a patient's previously agreed care programme. At no time should it be used as a spontaneous reaction to a particular type of behaviour.

18.4 A decision to use any psychological treatment programme for an individual patient should be preceded by a full discussion with the professional staff concerned with the patient.

18.5 Such a programme should be regularly reviewed in the case of each patient, and abandoned if it has proved ineffective or otherwise modified if necessary.

18.6 Patients and, with the patients' consent, their relatives, should be fully informed of the planned use of any such methods as part of a patient's treatment and the patient's consent should always be sought.

18.7 Psychological treatments may proceed in the absence of a patient's consent only where this is justified legally (see Chapters 15 and 16). If consent is not or cannot be given, and the patient is detained, or mentally incapacitated, a locally agreed procedure should be adopted in which the rmo should seek the advice of a suitably qualified person who is not a member of the clinical team responsible for the patient. This could be a psychologist, doctor, social worker or nurse who has received special training that equips them to supervise psychological procedures.

18.8 The rmo can authorise other members of staff to use such programmes. It remains the rmo's responsibility to ensure that those who are so authorised have adequate skills and abilities to carry out the procedures to the required standard. The Hospital Managers must ensure that such members of staff have received relevant training and have regular professional supervision.

Time out

18.9 Time out is a behaviour modification technique which denies a patient, for a period of no more than 15 minutes, opportunities to participate in an activity or to obtain positive reinforcers immediately following an incident of unacceptable behaviour. The patient is then returned to his or her original environment. Time out should never include the use of a locked room and should be clearly distinguished from seclusion which is for use in an emergency only and should never form part of a behavioural programme. Time out should:

- form part of a programme which enables the patient to achieve positive goals as well as reducing unwanted behaviour;
- enable a patient, following a change of behaviour, to be subject to fewer restrictions;
- ordinarily not take place in a room which is used for seclusion on other occasions;
- be used only as part of a planned approach to managing a difficult or disturbed patient.

18.10 Hospitals should have clear written policies about the use of time out. These should include a clear definition of this form of therapy and procedures for noting and monitoring its use on individual patients.

19 Patients presenting particular management problems

19.1 Patients, or people who may become patients, may behave in such a way as to disturb others around them, or their behaviour may present a risk to themselves or others around them or those charged with their care. These problems may occur anywhere, and the issues addressed here relate to general health care settings as well as to psychiatric facilities. It is important to distinguish:

- the needs of patients who pose an immediate threat to themselves or those around them and where techniques for the immediate management and control of a difficult situation must be used; and

- the need for some patients to remain in a secure environment as a result of a perceived risk to the general public or as a result of pending or past decisions of the courts, but who pose no immediate threat to those around them.

Behaviour contributing to problems in management

19.2 Patients' behaviour should be seen in its context. Professionals should not categorise behaviour as disturbed without taking account of the circumstances under which it occurs or assume that a previous history of disturbance means the patient will behave that way again. However they should also recognise that though they may experience the disturbed behaviour as intermittent, fellow residents or carers will experience it through 24 hours.

19.3 Behaviour which can give rise to managerial problems can include:

- refusal to participate in treatment programmes;

- prolonged verbal abuse and threatening behaviour;
- destructive behaviour;
- self-injurious behaviour;
- physical attacks on others;
- going missing.

Possible causes

19.4 In exploring preventive methods staff should be aware of some possible, often very evident causes of problem behaviours:

- boredom and lack of environmental stimulation;
- too much stimulation, noise and general disruption;
- overcrowding;
- antagonism, aggression or provocation on the part of others;
- influence of alcohol or substance abuse;
- an unsuitable mix of patients;
- the rewarding of undesirable behaviour by attention.

General preventive measures

19.5 In addition to individual care plans much can be done to prevent behaviour problems by examining the ward or other environment and pinpointing problem areas. Among such general measures are:

- keeping patients fully informed of what is happening and why;
- giving each patient a defined personal space and a secure locker for the safe keeping of possessions;
- ensuring access to open space;
- organising the ward (in hospital) to provide quiet rooms, recreation rooms, single sex areas and visitors' rooms;
- providing all necessary help for patients with any type of disability or impairment;
- ensuring access to a telephone;
- providing structured activities by professional staff;

- seeking patients' co-operation, and encouraging their participation in the general running of the ward;
- identifying those patients most at risk and ensuring appropriate levels of observation;
- encouraging energetic activities for younger patients;
- providing training for staff in the management of disturbed behaviour, including de-escalation techniques, diversional therapies and other non-physical intervention skills;
- monitoring the skill mix of staff;
- monitoring the mix of patients;
- developing a therapeutic relationship between each patient and a key worker/nurse;
- consistent application and monitoring of any individual programme;
- ensuring that patients' complaints are dealt with quickly and fairly.

Restraint

19.6 Restraint may take many forms. It may be both verbal and physical and may vary in degree from an instruction to seclusion. The purposes of restraint are:

- to take immediate control of a dangerous situation;
- to contain or limit the patient's freedom for no longer than is necessary; and
- to end or reduce significantly the danger to the patient or others.

The most common reasons for restraint are:

- physical assault;
- dangerous threatening or destructive behaviour;
- non-compliance with treatment;
- self-harm or risk of physical injury by accident;
- extreme and prolonged over-activity likely to lead to physical exhaustion.

19.7 The basic considerations which should underlie any methods aimed at reducing and eliminating unacceptable behaviour should take account of:

- the need for individual care planning;
- the physical condition of the patient;
- the physical environment of the ward or unit;
- the need to maintain adequate staffing levels.

Where the risk of problem behaviour is identified in a group of patients, but its onset cannot be predicted, an agreed strategy for dealing with such behaviour should be developed. This should include continuing risk assessment and management.

19.8 If the patient is not detained but restraint in any form has been deemed necessary, whether as an emergency or as part of the patient's treatment plan, consideration should be given to whether formal detention under the Act is appropriate, especially if restraint has occurred on a repeated basis.

Training

19.9 Staff in NHS hospitals and private mental nursing homes who are ordinarily likely to find themselves in situations where training in the management of actual or potential aggression might be necessary should attend an appropriate course taught by a qualified trainer. The trainer should have completed an appropriate course of preparation designed for health care settings and preferably validated by one of the health care bodies (English National Board or Royal College of Nursing Institute).

Methods of restraining behaviour

19.10 Physical restraint should be used as little as possible. Restraint which involves tying (whether by means of tape or by using a part of the patient's garments) to some part of a building or to its fixtures or fittings should never be used. Staff must make a balanced judgment between the need to promote an individual's autonomy by allowing him or her to move around at will and the duty to protect that person from likely harm. Where physical restraint is used staff should:

- record the decision and the reasons for it;
- state explicitly in a care plan under what circumstances restraint may be used;
- record what form the restraint may take and how its application will be reviewed; and
- document and review every episode of restraint.

19.11 Restraining aggressive behaviour by physical means should be done only as a last resort and never as a matter of course. It should be used in an emergency when there seems to be a real possibility that significant harm would occur if no intervention is made. Any initial attempt to restrain aggressive behaviour should, as far as the situation will allow, be non-physical:

a. assistance should be sought by call system or orally;

b. one member of the team should assume control of the incident;

c. the patient should be approached where possible and agreement sought to stop the behaviour, or to comply with a request. Approaches to deaf and hearing impaired patients should be made within their visual field (not from behind) and gestures used to engage them in calm communication;

d. where possible an explanation should be given of the consequences of refusing the request from staff to desist;

e. other patients or people not involved in the use of restraint should be asked to leave the area quietly.

19.12 A large number of staff acting in an uncoordinated way in attempting to restrain a patient can be counter-productive whereas fewer, but well briefed staff are likely to be more effective. If non-physical methods have failed or immediate action is needed, the person in control of the incident may decide to use physical restraint and should organise a small number of staff members to assist in managing the incident. Any restraint used should:

- be reasonable in the circumstances;
- apply the minimum force necessary to prevent harm to the patient or others;

- be used for only as long as is absolutely necessary;
- be sensitive to gender and race issues.

In doing so staff should:

a. make a visual check for weapons;
b. aim at restraining arms and legs from behind if possible, and seek to immobilise swiftly and safely;
c. continuously explain the reason for sustaining the action;
d. enlist support from the patient for voluntary control as soon as possible. If the patient is deaf or hearing impaired he or she must be able to see the staff member in control of the incident so that the attempt to communicate can be sustained;
e. not use neck holds;
f. avoid excess weight being placed on any area, but particularly on stomach and neck;
h. not slap, kick or punch.

Post-incident analysis and support should be developed for both staff and patients.

Restraint and complaints

19.13 The Hospital Managers should appoint a senior officer who should:

- be informed of any patient who is being subjected to any form of restraint that lasts for more than two hours;
- see the patient as soon as possible;
- visit and talk to the patient about the incident and ascertain if he or she has any concerns or complaints and if so assist in putting them forward.

The senior officer may delegate this task to a member of staff who has a good relationship with the patient.

Policy on restraint

19.14 All providers should have clear, written policies on the use of restraint of which all staff should be aware. The policy should include provision for review of each incident of restraint, and its application should be audited and reported to the Hospital Managers.

Medication

19.15 Medication to reduce excitement and activity may be useful to facilitate other therapeutic interventions. Other than in exceptional circumstances, the control of behaviour by medication should only be used after careful consideration, and as part of a treatment plan (see Chapters 15 and 16). Medication which is given for therapeutic reasons may become a method of restraint if used routinely for prolonged periods. Before medication is given, the doctor in charge should consider whether it would be lawful and therapeutic in the longer term. Medication should never be used to manage patients in the absence of adequate staffing.

Seclusion

19.16 Seclusion is the supervised confinement of a patient in a room, which may be locked to protect others from significant harm. Its sole aim is to contain severely disturbed behaviour which is likely to cause harm to others.

Seclusion should be used:

* as a last resort;
* for the shortest possible time.

Seclusion should not be used:

* as a punishment or threat;
* as part of a treatment programme;
* because of shortage of staff;
* where there is any risk of suicide or self-harm.

Seclusion of an informal patient should be taken as an indicator of the need to consider formal detention.

19.17 Hospitals should have clear written guidelines on the use of seclusion which:

- ensure the safety and well being of the patient;
- ensure the patient receives the care and support rendered necessary by his or her seclusion both during and after it has taken place;
- distinguish between seclusion and 'time-out' (see paras 18.9-18.10);
- specify a suitable environment taking account of patient's dignity and physical well being;
- set out the roles and responsibilities of staff;
- set requirements for recording, monitoring, reviewing the use of seclusion and any follow-up action.

Procedure for seclusion

19.18 The decision to use seclusion can be made in the first instance by a doctor or the nurse in charge. Where the decision is taken by someone other than a doctor, the rmo or duty doctor should be notified at once and should attend immediately unless the seclusion is only for a very brief period (no more than five minutes).

19.19 A nurse should be readily available within sight and sound of the seclusion room at all times throughout the period of the patient's seclusion, and present at all times with a patient who has been sedated.

19.20 The aim of observation is to monitor the condition and behaviour of the patient and to identify the time at which seclusion can be terminated. The level should be decided on an individual basis and the patient should be observed continuously. A documented report must be made at least every 15 minutes.

19.21 The need to continue seclusion should be reviewed

- every 2 hours by 2 nurses (1 of whom was not involved in the decision to seclude), and
- every 4 hours by a doctor.

A multidisciplinary review should be completed by a consultant or other senior doctor, nurses and other professionals, who were not involved in the incident which led to the seclusion if the seclusion continues for more than:

- 8 hours consecutively; or
- 12 hours intermittently over a period of 48 hours.

If the need for seclusion is disputed by any member of the multidisciplinary team, the matter should be referred to a senior manager.

Conditions of seclusion

19.22 The room used for seclusion should:

- provide privacy from other patients;
- enable staff to observe the patient at all times;
- be safe and secure;
- not contain anything which could cause harm to the patient or others;
- be adequately furnished, heated, lit and ventilated;
- be quiet but not soundproofed and with some means of calling for attention; the means of operation should be explained to the patient.

Staff may decide what a patient may take into the seclusion room, but the patient should always be clothed.

Record keeping

19.23 Detailed and contemporaneous records should be kept in the patient's case notes of any use of seclusion, the reasons for its use and subsequent activity, cross-referenced to a special seclusion book or forms which should contain a step-by-step account of the seclusion procedure in every instance. The principal entry should be made by the nurse in charge of the ward and the record should be countersigned by a doctor and a senior nurse. The Hospital Managers should monitor and regularly review the use of seclusion.

Locking ward doors on open wards

19.24 The management, security and safety of patients should be ensured by means of adequate staffing. Service providers are responsible for ensuring that staffing is adequate to prevent the need for the practice of locking patients in wards, individual rooms or any other area.

19.25 The nurse in charge of any shift is responsible for the care and protection of patients and staff and the maintenance of a safe environment. This responsibility includes the care of patients who have been detained in hospital because they are considered a danger to other people. The nurse in charge of a shift has discretion for all or part of that shift to lock the door of the ward, to protect patients or others, because of the behaviour of a patient or patients. The nurse in charge should:

a. inform all staff of why this action is being taken, how long it will last and a notice to that effect should be displayed at the entrance to the ward;

b. inform the patient or patients whose behaviour has led to the ward door being locked of the reasons for taking such action;

c. inform all other patients that they may leave on request at any time and ensure that someone is available to unlock the door;

d. inform his or her line manager of the action taken;

e. inform the rmo or nominated deputy;

f. keep a record of this action and reasons, and make use of an incident reporting procedure.

19.26 When handing over to the relieving shift the nurse in charge should discuss in detail the reasons for the action taken. Where the relieving nurse considers it necessary to keep the door locked, (a) to (f) above apply. Where any ward is locked for three consecutive shifts (excluding night duty) the senior manager responsible for that ward should be informed.

19.27 The safety of informal patients who would be at risk of harm if they wandered out of a ward or mental nursing home at will, should be ensured by adequate staffing and good supervision. Combination locks and double handed doors should be used only in units where there is a regular and significant risk of patients wandering off accidentally and being at risk of harm. There should be clear policies on the use of locks and other devices and a mechanism for reviewing decisions. Every patient should have an individual care plan which states explicitly why and when he or she will be prevented from leaving the ward. Patients who are not deliberately trying to leave the ward, but who may wander out accidentally, may legitimately be deterred from leaving the ward by those devices. In the case of a patient who persistently and/or purposely attempts to leave a ward or mental nursing home, whether or not they understand the risk involved, consideration must be given to assessing whether they would more appropriately be formally detained under the Act in a hospital or a mental nursing home registered to take detained patients, than remain as informal patients (see Chapter 2).

Locked wards and secure areas

19.28 There are some detained patients in general psychiatric hospitals and mental nursing homes who may be liable to cause danger to themselves or others. For these patients professional judgment, or the requirement of a Court as an alternative to imprisonment, may point to the need for varying degrees of security. In such cases, where the need for physical security is a prerequisite, the patient's rmo, in consultation with the multi-disciplinary team, should ensure that:

a. he or she has carefully weighed the patient's individual circumstances and the degree of danger involved;

b. he or she has assessed the relative clinical considerations of placing the patient in a physically secure environment, in addition to or as opposed to providing care by way of intensive staffing;

c. treatment in secure conditions lasts for the minimum necessary period;

d. arrangements are made to enable his or her speedy return to an open ward when physical security is no longer required.

19.29 Service providers should ensure that:

a. a ward/area is specifically designated for this purpose with adequate staffing levels;

b. written guidelines are provided, setting out:

- the categories of patient for whom it is appropriate to use physically secure conditions;
- those for whom it is not appropriate;
- a clear policy for practice, procedure and safeguards for treatment in secure conditions.

Observation, care and management of patients at risk of self injury

19.30 Patients must be protected from harming themselves when the drive to self injury is a result of mental disorder for which they are receiving care and treatment. On admission, all patients should be assessed for immediate and potential risks of going missing, suicide, self harm and self neglect, taking into account their social and clinical history. Individual care plans should include:

- a clear statement of the degree of risk of self harm;
- the measures required to manage the risk safely;
- the level of observation needed to ensure the patient's safety.

Staff must balance the potentially distressing effect on the patient of close observation, particularly when one-to-one observation is proposed for many hours, against the risk of self injury. Levels of observation and risk should be regularly reviewed and a record made of agreed decisions.

19.31 Staff should observe changes in the patient's:

- general behaviour;
- movement;
- posture;
- speech;
- expression of ideas;
- appearance;
- orientation;
- mood and attitude;
- interaction with others;
- reaction to medication.

Deprivation of daytime clothing

19.32 Patients should never be deprived of appropriate daytime clothing during the day, with the intention of restricting their freedom of movement. They should not be deprived of other aids necessary for their daily living.

Staff

19.33 Staff must try to gain the confidence of patients so that they can learn to recognise potential danger signs. Staff should understand when to intervene to prevent harm from occurring. Continuity of staffing is an important factor both in the development of professional skills and consistency in managing patients.

Management responsibilities

19.34 Staff who take part in incidents involving control and restraint may experience a degree of stress. Hospital Managers should ensure that they are given the opportunity to discuss these issues with them (the managers) and with colleagues. Hospital Managers should formulate and make available to staff a clear written operational policy on all forms of restraint, including post-incident analysis and support for patients and staff.

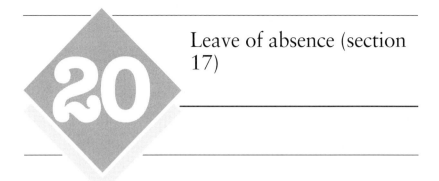

Leave of absence (section 17)

20.1 A patient who is currently liable to be detained in a hospital or a specified hospital unit, can only leave that hospital, or hospital unit, lawfully - even for a very short period - by being given leave of absence in accordance with the provisions of section 17 or by way of transfer to another hospital under section 19. Leave of absence can be an important part of a patient's treatment plan. Only the patient's rmo, with the approval of the Home Secretary in the case of restricted patients, can grant a detained patient leave of absence. Rmos are not entitled to grant leave of absence to patients detained under sections 35, 36 or 38. Except where the patient is detained in a specified hospital unit, no formal procedures are needed to allow a patient to go to different parts of the hospital or hospital grounds as part of the care programme.

20.2 Leave of absence can be granted by the rmo for specific occasions or for longer indefinite or specific periods of time. The period of leave may be extended in the patient's absence. The granting of leave should not be used as an alternative to discharging the patient.

20.3 **The power to grant leave (section 17)**

a.   Unrestricted patients

The rmo cannot delegate the decision to grant leave of absence to any other doctor or professional. The rmo is responsible for undertaking any appropriate consultation, and may make leave subject to conditions which he or she considers necessary in the interests of the patient or for the protection of other people. Only the rmo can grant leave of absence to a patient formally detained under the Act. In the absence of the rmo (for example, if he or she is on annual leave or otherwise unavailable) permission can only be granted by the doctor who is for the time being in charge of the patient's treatment. Where practicable this should be another consultant psychiatrist, a locum consultant or specialist registrar approved under section 12(2) of the Act. The granting of leave cannot be vetoed by the Hospital Managers.

b.   Restricted patients

Any proposal to grant leave has to be approved by the Home Secretary who should be given as much notice as possible, together with full details of the proposed leave.

Short-term leave

20.4 The rmo, with the authority of the Home Secretary if the patient is subject to restrictions, may decide to authorise short-term local leave, which may be managed by other staff. For example, the patient may be given leave for a shopping trip of two hours every week, with the decision on the particular two hours left to the discretion of the responsible nursing staff. It is crucial that such decisions fall within the terms of the grant of periodic leave by the rmo, and that he or she reviews decisions and their implementation from time to time and explicitly records the outcome in writing (see para 20.6).

Longer periods of leave

20.5 Leave of absence should be properly planned, if possible well in advance. Leave may be used to assess an unrestricted patient's suitability for discharge from detention. The patient should be fully involved in the decision to grant leave and should be able to demonstrate to the professional carers that he or she is likely to cope outside the hospital. Subject to the patient's consent there should be detailed consultation with any appropriate relatives or friends (especially where the patient is to reside with them) and with community services. Leave should not be granted if the patient does not consent to relatives or friends who are to be involved in his or her care being consulted.

Recording and information

20.6 The granting of leave and the conditions attached to it should be recorded in the patient's notes and copies given to the patient, any appropriate relatives or friends and any professionals in the community who need to know. Hospitals should adopt a local record form on which the rmo can authorise leave and specify the conditions attached to it.

Care and treatment while on leave

20.7 The rmo's responsibilities for the patient's care remain the same while he or she is on leave although they are exercised in a different way. The duty to provide after-care under section 117 includes patients who are on leave of absence.

20.8 A patient granted leave under section 17 remains 'liable to be detained' and the provisions of Part IV of the Act continue to apply. If it becomes necessary to administer treatment in the absence of the patient's consent under Part IV, consideration should be given to recalling the patient to hospital. The refusal of treatment would not on its own be sufficient grounds for recall (see para 20.11). Such a recall direction should be in writing.

Patients in custody or in other hospitals

20.9 The rmo may direct that the patient remains in custody while on leave of absence, either in the patient's own interests or for the protection of other people. The patient may be kept in the custody of any officer on the staff of the hospital or of any person authorised in writing by the Hospital Managers. Such an arrangement is often useful, for example, to enable patients to participate in escorted trips, or to have compassionate home leave.

20.10 The rmo may also require the patient, as a condition of leave, to reside at another hospital and he or she may then be kept in the custody of an officer of that hospital. The patient's detention can be renewed during a period of leave[12]. However, consideration should be given as to

---

[13] R v Managers of Warley Hospital ex parte Barker [1998] COD 309

whether it would be more appropriate to move the patient from one hospital to another under the provisions of section 19 rather than being given section 17 leave.

Recall to hospital

20.11 The rmo may revoke a patient's leave at any time if he or she considers this to be necessary in the interests of the patient's health or safety or for the protection of other people. The rmo must consider very seriously the reasons for recalling a patient and the effects this may have on him or her. For example a refusal to take medication would not on its own be a reason for revocation; the rmo would have to be satisfied that this was necessary in the patient's interests or for the safety of others. The rmo must arrange for a notice in writing revoking the leave to be served on the patient or on the person for the time being in charge of the patient. The reasons for recall should be fully explained to the patient and a record of such explanation placed in the patient's case notes. A restricted patient's leave may be revoked either by the rmo or the Home Secretary.

20.12 It is essential that any appropriate relatives and friends, especially where the patient is residing with them whilst on leave, and other professionals in the community who need to know should have easy access to the patient's rmo if they feel consideration should be given to the return of the patient to hospital before his or her leave is due to end.

Duration of leave/renewal of authority to detain

20.13 A period of leave cannot last longer than the duration of the authority to detain which was current when leave was granted. If the authority to detain an unrestricted patient might expire whilst the patient is on leave the rmo may examine the patient and consider writing a report renewing the detention when the patient is still on leave, if the rmo thinks that further formal in-patient treatment is necessary and the statutory criteria are met[13].

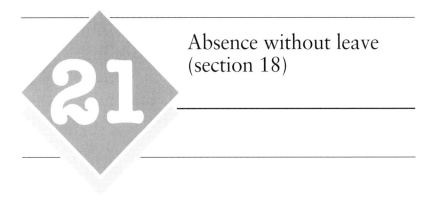

Absence without leave (section 18)

(paras 70-71 of the Memorandum)

21.1 Section 18 provides powers for the return of patients who are absent from hospital without leave, fail to return to hospital at the end of an authorised leave of absence or when recalled, or are absent without permission from an address where they have been required to live either by the conditions of their leave of absence, or by their guardian. The hospital must know the address of a person on leave of absence.

21.2 A patient who is liable to be detained in hospital may be taken into custody and returned to hospital or the place where he or she is required to live by an ASW, any officer on the staff of the hospital, any police officer, or any person authorised in writing by the Hospital Managers.

21.3 A patient who has been required to reside in another hospital as a condition of leave of absence can also be taken into custody by any officer on the staff of that hospital or by any person authorised by the managers of that hospital. Otherwise responsibility for the safe return of the patient rests with the detaining hospital. If the absconding patient is initially taken to another hospital that hospital may, if authorised by the managers of the detaining hospital in writing, detain the patient while arrangements are made for his or return. Such authority can be provided by fax.

21.4 A person absent without leave while under guardianship may be taken into custody by any officer on the staff of the local social services authority, or by any person authorised in writing by the guardian or the local social services authority.

Local policies

21.5 It is the responsibility of the Hospital Managers, and of the local Social Services Authority where guardianship is concerned, to ensure that there is a clear written policy in relation to action to be taken when a detained patient or a person subject to guardianship goes absent without leave. All staff should be familiar with this policy.

21.6 The policy should include guidance as to:

a. the immediate action to be taken by any member of staff who becomes aware that a patient has gone absent without leave, including the requirement that they immediately inform the nurse in charge of the patient's ward who should in turn ensure that the patient's rmo is immediately informed;

b. the circumstances when a search of the hospital and its grounds should be initiated;

c. the circumstances when other local agencies with an interest, including the social services authority, should be notified, in the case of a patient detained in hospital;

d. the circumstances when the police should be informed, in the case of a patient detained in hospital. This should be the subject of agreed local arrangements with the police. The police should be asked to assist in returning a patient to hospital only if necessary, but they should always be informed immediately of the absence without leave of a patient who is considered to be vulnerable, dangerous or who is subject to restrictions under Part III of the Act. There may be other cases where, although the help of the police is not needed, a patient's history makes it desirable to inform them that he or she is absent without leave in the area. Whenever the police are asked for help in returning a patient they must be informed of the time limit for taking him or her into custody;

e. how and when the patient's nearest relative should be informed. In almost all cases the patient's nearest relative should be informed immediately the patient goes absent without leave and any exceptions to this requirement should be clearly set out in the policy;

f.   the action that should be taken in the case of someone received into guardianship who is absent without leave from the place where he or she is required to reside. This should include immediate notification of the specified guardian and the social services authority.

Duties of the Hospital Managers

22.1 The Hospital Managers have a central role in operating the provisions of the Act. In England and Wales, in general, NHS Hospitals are owned by NHS trusts. For these hospitals the Trusts themselves are defined as the "managers" for the purposes of the Act. But the three special hospitals are owned by the Secretary of State and Hospital Managers' functions are exercised on behalf of the Secretary of State by the Special Health Authorities which have been set up to manage those hospitals as Special Hospital Authorities. In the case of a mental nursing home the person or persons in whose name the home is registered are managers for the purposes of the Act.

22.2 It is the Hospital Managers who have the power to detain patients who have been admitted under the Act. They have the key responsibility for seeing that the requirements of the Act are followed. In particular they must ensure that patients are detained only as the Act allows, that their treatment and care accord fully with its provisions, and that they are fully informed of, and are supported in exercising, their statutory rights.

22.3 The main responsibilities which the Act confers on the Hospital Managers are set out in paras 22.7-22.16. More detailed guidance is given in the relevant chapters of the Code. The exercise of the Hospital Managers' powers to discharge patients is dealt with in Chapter 23.

Exercise of the Hospital Managers' functions

22.4 The Trust or Hospital Authority should appoint a committee or sub-committee to undertake the Hospital Managers' functions. The legislation allows such a committee to be made up of Directors of the Trust or Hospital Authority, or outside people, or a mixture of the two. Most of the Hospital Managers' responsibilities may be delegated to officers of the Trust or Hospital Authority but the power to discharge patients may only be exercised by three or more committee members who are not also employees of the Trust (see Chapter 23). The Hospital Managers retain responsibility for the performance of all delegated duties and must ensure that those acting on their behalf are competent to undertake them.

22.5 The Trust or Hospital Authority retains the ultimate responsibility for the performance of the Hospital Managers' duties, and in view of this the committee should, where possible, include members of the Trust or Hospital Authority Board. The committee should report formally to the Board with an account of its activities not less than once a year. Trusts and Hospital Authorities must ensure that all those appointed to exercise the Hospital Managers' functions are properly informed about the working of the Act and receive suitable training in their role. Such appointments should be made for a fixed period and any reappointments should be preceded by a review.

22.6 For detained patients placed in a mental nursing home under a contract with a Trust, the Trust committee which is appointed to undertake Hospital Managers' functions should also monitor the way those functions are performed by the managers of the mental nursing home.

Specific duties

Admission

22.7 It is the Hospital Managers' duty to ensure that the grounds for admitting the patient are valid and that all relevant admission documents are in order. Any officer to whom the responsibility is delegated must be competent to make such a judgment, and to identify any error in the documents which may require rectification. Guidance on the receipt, scrutiny and rectification of documents is given in chapter 12 and *paras 44-54 of the Memorandum.*

22.8 Where a patient is admitted under the Act following an application by his or her nearest relative, the Hospital Managers should request the relevant local social services department to provide them with the social circumstances report required by section 14.

Transfer between hospitals

22.9 Section 19 of the Act, and the regulations[13] made under it allow the Hospital Managers to transfer a detained patient from one hospital to another. Officers to whom this responsibility is delegated must ensure that the transfer is being made for valid reasons and that the needs and interests of the patient have been fully considered. For restricted patients, the Hospital Managers' power is subject to the prior agreement of the Home Secretary.

Discharge

22.10 Section 23 provides for the rmo to discharge a detained patient by giving an order in writing. The Hospital Managers should ensure that a suitable form is available upon which this order can be given and that it is received and acknowledged by someone authorised to receive and scrutinise documents on their behalf.

22.11 The exercise of the Hospital Managers' own powers to discharge patients is dealt with in Chapter 23.

Information for health and local authorities

22.12 Where a Tribunal hearing has been arranged, the Hospital Managers should inform Health and Local Authorities so that they are able to consider the need for a section 117 care planning meeting before the Tribunal takes place and, if necessary, provide a report to the Tribunal (see para 27.7).

Information for patients and relatives

22.13 Sections 132 and 133 require the Hospital Managers to give certain information to detained patients and their relatives. Guidance on the exercise of this duty is given in Chapter 14.

---

[13] Regulations 7 and 9 of the Mental Health (Hospital, Guardianship and Consent to Treatment) Regulations 1983 (S.I. 1983 NO. 893) amended by the Mental Health (Hospital, Guardianship and Consent to Treatment) (Amendment) Regulations 1996 (S.I. 1996/540)

Correspondence of patients

22.14 Section 134 allows the Hospital Managers to withhold outgoing mail from detained patients if the addressee has requested this in writing to the Hospital Managers, the patient's rmo or the Secretary of State. The fact that mail has been withheld must be recorded in writing and the patient must be informed.

22.15 The Hospital Managers of the special hospitals have wider powers under section 134 to withhold both incoming and outgoing mail from patients in certain circumstances. This is subject to review by the Mental Health Act Commission. The Hospital Managers of the special hospitals should have a written policy for the exercise of these powers which should be discussed with the Commission.

Access to Mental Health Review Tribunals

22.16 If a patient, or the patient's nearest relative, does not exercise his or her right to apply to a Mental Health Review Tribunal, section 68 requires the Hospital Managers to refer a patient's case to the Tribunal:

a. when six months have elapsed since the patient was admitted under section 3 or transferred from guardianship under section 19 if the patient has not applied for a Tribunal during the first six months (this does not apply to patients admitted under a hospital order or transferred from prison to hospital); and

b. at the time when the patient's detention is renewed if he or she has not then had a Tribunal review for three years or more; this applies also to unrestricted patients admitted under a hospital order or prison transfer direction.

The reference should be made within one week of the patient's detention being renewed.

22.17 The Hospital Managers should ensure that a patient who wishes to apply to a Tribunal is given all necessary help with his or her application.

22.18 The Hospital Managers should ensure that when a Tribunal hearing has been arranged officers of the Trust provide reports (including any reports about after-care) to the Tribunal within the time limits set in the Tribunal rules.

The Hospital Managers' power of discharge (section 23)

23.1 Section 23 gives the Hospital Managers (see para 22.1) the power to discharge an unrestricted patient from detention. Discharge of a restricted patient requires the consent of the Home Secretary. The power may be exercised on behalf of the Hospital Managers by three or more members of a committee or sub-committee formed for that purpose. In the case of a Trust or Hospital Authority the committee or sub-committee must not include any employee or officer of the Trust or Hospital Authority concerned.

Principles

23.2 The legislation does not define either the criteria or the procedure for reviewing a patient's detention. However the exercise of this power is subject to the general law and to public law duties which arise from it. The Hospital Managers' conduct of reviews must satisfy the fundamental legal requirements of fairness, reasonableness and lawfulness:

a. they must adopt and apply a procedure which is fair and reasonable;

b. they must not make irrational decisions, that is, decisions which no body of Hospital Managers, properly directing themselves as to the law and on the available information, could have made; and

c. they must not act unlawfully, that is, contrary to the provisions of the Act, any other legislation and any applicable regulations.

Review panels

23.3 The Trust or Hospital Authority retains the final responsibility for the proper performance of the Hospital Managers' duties in considering whether or not patients should be discharged. To reflect this the review panel should, if possible, include a non-executive member of the Board. The panel must have at least three members. The Board must ensure that all those appointed to this role are properly informed and experienced and receive suitable training (see also para 22.5).

23.4 The person or persons registered in respect of a mental nursing home (see para 22.1) retain final responsibility for the performance of the Hospital Managers' duties in considering whether or not patients should be discharged. They may delegate their discharge function to a committee or sub-committee. It is desirable that detention is reviewed by people who are neither on the staff of the home nor have a financial interest.

23.5 Mental nursing home managers, and Trusts and Health Authorities should, where possible, co-operate over exercising their respective functions in relation to the discharge of patients detained in mental nursing homes.

When to review

23.6 The Hospital Managers should ensure that all patients are aware that they may seek discharge by the Hospital Managers and of the distinction between this and their right to a Mental Health Review Tribunal hearing.

23.7 The Hospital Managers may undertake a review at any time at their discretion, but they must review a patient's detention when the rmo submits a report under section 20(3) renewing detention. Such reports should normally be submitted not less than two weeks before the current period of detention expires, to enable the review to take place as close as possible to the expiry date.

23.8 The Hospital Managers must consider holding a review:

a.   when they receive a request from a patient;

b.   when the rmo makes a report under section 25(1) opposing a nearest relative's application for the patient's discharge.

23.9 The Hospital Managers should consider carefully whether it is appropriate to hold a review in the case of patients detained for treatment, if there has been a review in the last 28 days and there is no evidence that the patient's condition has changed or a Mental Health Review Tribunal hearing is due in the next 28 days.

23.10 In the cases covered by para 23.8a and b above the patient, or nearest relative, will be actively seeking his or her discharge. In the case where the rmo submits a report renewing detention, the Hospital Managers are under a statutory obligation to consider the renewal even if the patient does not object to it. The procedures adopted need to differentiate "uncontested" renewals from reviews where detention is contested by the patient (see paras 23.13-23.19).

Criteria

23.11 The Act does not define specific criteria to be applied by the Hospital Managers when considering the discharge of a patient who is detained or liable to be detained. The essential yardstick in considering a review application is whether the grounds for admission or continued detention under the Act are satisfied. To ensure that this is done in a systematic and consistent way the review panel should consider the following questions, in the order stated:

- Is the patient still suffering from mental disorder?
- If so, is the disorder of a nature or degree which makes treatment in a hospital appropriate?
- Is detention in hospital still necessary in the interests of the patient's health or safety, or for the protection of other people?

If the panel is satisfied from the evidence presented to them that the answer to any of these questions is "no", the patient should be discharged.

23.12 In cases where the rmo has made a report under section 25(1), the managers should not only consider the three questions above but also the following question:

- Would the patient, if discharged, be likely to act in a manner dangerous to other persons or to him or herself?[14]

This question focuses on the probability of dangerous acts, such as causing serious physical injury, not merely the patient's general need for safety and others' general need for protection: it provides a more stringent test for continuing detention. If, on consideration of the report under section 25(1) and other evidence, the managers disagree with the rmo and decide the answer to this question is "no", they should usually discharge the patient.

Conduct of reviews - where detention is contested

23.13 The review should be conducted so as to ensure that the case for discharging, or continuing to detain, the patient is properly considered against the above criteria and in the light of all relevant evidence. This means that the review panel needs to have before it sufficient information about the patient's past history of care and treatment, and details of any future plans. The main source of this will be the patient's CPA documentation or care plan. It is essential that the panel is fully informed about any history of violence or self-harm, and any risk assessment which has been conducted.

23.14 In advance of the hearing the review panel should obtain written reports from the patient's rmo and others who are directly involved in the patient's care such as the key worker, named nurse, social worker and clinical psychologist. The patient should receive copies of the reports unless the Hospital Managers are of the opinion that the information disclosed would be likely to cause serious harm to the physical or mental health of the patient or any other individual. The patient's nearest or most concerned relatives, and any informal carer should be informed of the review, if the patient consents. Relatives and carers may be invited to put their views to the panel in person. If the patient objects to this a suitable member of the professional care team should be asked to include the relatives' and/or carer's views in his or her report.

23.15 The report submitted by the rmo should cover the history of the patient's care and treatment and details of his or her CPA or care plan,

---

[14] R v Riverside Mental Health NHS Trust ex parte Huzzey [1998]

including all risk assessments. Where there is a rmo report under section 20 renewing detention (form 30) the panel should also have a copy of it before them. This should be supplemented by a record of the consultation undertaken by the rmo in accordance with section 20(5). The written reports should be considered by the panel alongside the documentation compiled under the CPA.

23.16 The procedure for the conduct of the hearing is for the Hospital Managers to decide, but generally it needs to balance informality against the rigour demanded by the importance of the task. Key points are:

- The patient should be given a full opportunity, and any necessary help, to explain why he or she wishes to be discharged.

- The patient should be allowed to be accompanied by a friend or representative of his or her own choosing to help in putting his or her point of view to the panel.

- The rmo and other professionals should be asked to give their views on:
  - whether the patient's continued detention is justified; and
  - the factors on which those views are based.

- The patient and the other parties to the review should, if the patient wishes it, be able to hear each other's statements to the panel and to put questions to each other. However the patient should always be offered the opportunity of speaking to the panel alone.

23.17 While the panel must give full weight to the views of all the professionals concerned in the patient's care its members will not, as a rule, be qualified to form clinical assessments of their own. If there is a divergence of views about whether the patient meets the clinical grounds for continued detention, especially in relation to matters such as risk assessment, the panel should consider an adjournment to seek further medical or other professional advice.

23.18 In applying the criteria in para 23.11 and 23.12, and deciding in the light of them whether or not to discharge the patient, the panel needs to consider very carefully the implications for the patient's subsequent care. The presence or absence of adequate community care arrangements may be critical in deciding whether continued detention is necessary in the interests of the patient's health or safety or for the protection of others. If the panel conclude that the patient ought to be discharged but arrangements for after-care need to be made, they may adjourn the panel, for a brief period, to enable a full CPA/care planning meeting to take place.

Decision

23.19 The Hospital Managers' decision following the review, and the reasons for it, should be recorded. The decision should be communicated immediately, both orally and in writing, to the patient, to the nearest relative with the patient's consent, and to the professionals concerned. At least one of the members of the panel should see the patient to explain in person the reasons for the decision. Copies of the papers relating to the review, and the formal record of the decision, should be placed in the patient's records.

Uncontested renewals

23.20 If a patient's detention is renewed under section 20, and the patient has indicated that he or she does not object to this, the review panel should meet to consider the papers and should interview the patient and his or her key worker. If the panel then agree that the patient should not be discharged the review can be concluded and the outcome recorded in the patient's records.

Complaints

24.1 Guidance on the arrangements introduced in April 1996 for dealing with complaints about NHS treatment and services is contained in the document *Complaints: Listening ...Acting...Improving. Guidance on implementation of the NHS Complaints Procedure (EL(96) 19)*, and parallel guidance issued in Wales in March 1996. All providers of NHS services have been directed under the Hospital Complaints and Procedures Act 1985 to have complaints handling arrangements in place.

24.2 Trusts and Authorities are responsible for ensuring that staff are adequately trained in the requirements and procedures of the new system, and in dealing with complaints. Staff have the responsibly of bringing to the attention of all patients, both orally and in writing, the procedures for making a complaint through the NHS complaints system, and, in relation to detained patients, their rights to complain to the Mental Health Act Commission. If a patient is unable to formulate a complaint, he or she should be given reasonable assistance to do so by staff. It is the personal responsibility of all members of staff involved in a patient's care to give such assistance where necessary.

Recording

24.3 The guidance on the NHS complaints system states that as a matter of good practice complaints records should be kept separate from health records. Patients' health records should contain only information which is strictly relevant to their care and treatment.

Personal searches

25.1 Managers of hospitals and mental nursing homes admitting patients under the Act should ensure that there is an operational policy on the searching of patients and their belongings. The policy should be based on legal advice.

25.2 The purpose of the policy is to meet two objectives which may, at least in part, be in conflict: firstly the creation and maintenance of a therapeutic environment in which treatment may take place; and secondly, the maintenance of the security of the establishment and the safety of patients, staff and the public.

25.3 The policy may extend to routine and random searching without cause, but only in exceptional circumstances, for example, where the dangerous or violent criminal propensities of patients create a self evident and pressing need for additional security[15].

25.4 In all cases, the consent of the patient should be sought before a search is attempted. If consent is duly given, the search should be carried out with due regard for the dignity of the individual and the need to ensure maximum privacy.

25.5 If consent is refused, the rmo for the patient should first be contacted so that any clinical objection to a search by force may be raised. If no such objection is raised, the search should proceed as set out in para 25.8.

---

[15] R v Broadmoor Special Hospital Authority ex parte S [1998] COD 199

25.6 If a clinical objection is raised by the rmo, but the person empowered to search wishes nonetheless to proceed, the matter should be referred to the medical director of the hospital for decision.

25.7 Any delay in respect of paragraphs 25.5 and 25.6 should be kept to a minimum. While the matter is being resolved, a patient should be kept under observation and isolated from other patients. The patient should be told what is happening and why, in terms appropriate to his or her understanding.

25.8 If a search is to proceed without consent, it should be carried out with due regard for the dignity of the individual and the need to ensure maximum privacy. The minimum force necessary should be used. A search of a patient's person should be carried out by a member of the same sex unless necessity dictates otherwise.

25.9 If items belonging to a patient are removed, the patient should be given a receipt for the items and informed where they are being kept.

Visiting patients detained in hospital or registered mental nursing homes

The right to be visited

26.1 All detained patients are entitled to maintain contact with and be visited by anyone they wish to see, subject only to some carefully limited exceptions. Maintaining contact with friends and relatives is recognised as an important element in a patient's treatment and rehabilitation. The decision to prohibit a visit by a person whom the patient has requested to visit or agreed to see should be regarded as a serious interference with the rights of the patient and to be taken only in exceptional circumstances. This should only occur after other means to deal with the problem have been exhausted. Any decision to exclude a visitor should be fully documented and available for independent scrutiny by the Mental Health Act Commission.

Grounds for excluding a visitor

26.2 There are two principal grounds which may justify the exclusion of a visitor:

a. Restriction on clinical grounds

It will sometimes be the case that a patient's relationship with a relative, friend or supporter is anti-therapeutic (in the short or long term) to an extent that discernible arrest of progress or even deterioration in the patient's mental state is evident and can reasonably be anticipated if contact were not to be restricted. Very occasionally, concern may centre primarily on the potential safety of a particular visitor to a disturbed patient. The grounds for any decision by the rmo, taken after full discussion with the patient's multi-disciplinary care team, should be clearly documented and explained to the patient and the person concerned, orally and in writing.

b. Restriction on security grounds

The behaviour of a particular visitor may be, or have been in the past, disruptive to a degree that exclusion from the hospital or mental nursing home is necessary as a last resort. Examples of such behaviour include: incitement to abscond, smuggling of illicit drugs/alcohol into the hospital, mental nursing home or unit, transfer of potential weapons, or unacceptable aggression or unauthorised media access. A decision to exclude a visitor on the grounds of his or her behaviour should be fully documented and explained to the patient orally and in writing. Where possible and appropriate the reason for the decision should be communicated to the person concerned.

Visiting of patients by children

26.3 Hospitals should have written policies on the arrangements about the visiting of patients by children, which should be drawn up in consultation with local social services authorities. A visit by a child should only take place following a decision that such a visit would be in the child's best interests. Decisions to allow such visits should be regularly reviewed.

Facilitation of visiting

26.4 The hospital or mental nursing home should be sufficiently flexible to enable regular visits to the patient, if he or she wishes. Ordinarily, inadequate staff numbers should not be allowed to deter regular visiting. The facilities provided for visitors should be comfortable and welcoming, and for children, child-friendly. Consideration should be given to meeting the needs of visitors who have travelled long distances.

Other forms of communication

26.5 Every effort must be made to assist the patient, where appropriate, to make contact with relatives, friends and supporters. In particular patients should have readily accessible and appropriate day time telephone facilities and no restrictions should be placed upon dispatch and receipt of their mail over and above those referred to in section 134 of the Act.

Hospital Managers

26.6 Hospital Managers should regularly monitor the exclusion from the hospital or mental nursing home of visitors to detained patients.

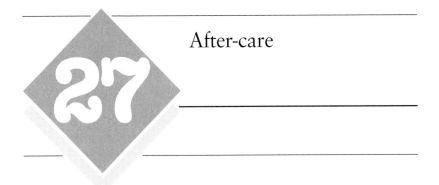

After-care

27.1 While the Act defines after-care requirements only in very broad terms, it is clear that a central purpose of all treatment and care is to equip patients to cope with life outside hospital and function there successfully without danger to themselves or other people. The planning of this needs to start when the patient is admitted to hospital.

27.2 These objectives apply to all patients receiving treatment and care from the specialist psychiatric services, whether or not they are admitted to hospital and whether or not they are detained under the Act. They are embodied in the Care Programme Approach (CPA) set out in Circular HC(90)23/LASSL(90)11, and in the Welsh Office Mental Illness Strategy (WHC(95)40). The key elements of the CPA are:

- systematic arrangements for assessing people's health and social care needs;
- the formulation of a care plan which addresses those needs;
- the appointment of a key worker to keep in close touch with the patient and monitor care;
- regular review and if need be, agreed changes to the care plan.

27.3 Section 117 of the Act requires Health Authorities and local Social Services Authorities, in conjunction with voluntary agencies, to provide after-care for certain categories of detained patients. This includes patients given leave of absence under section 17. The after-care of detained patients should be included in the general arrangements for implementing the CPA, but because of the specific statutory obligation it is important that all patients who are subject to section 117 are identified and records kept of them. There is a section 117 after-care entitlement when the patient stays in hospital informally after ceasing to be detained under the Act, and also when a patient is released from prison, if they have spent part of their sentence detained in hospital. There are special considerations to be taken into account in the case of patients who are subject to restrictions under Part III of the Act (see Chapter 29).

27.4 NHS Managers and Directors of Social Services should ensure that all staff are aware of the CPA and related provisions. Further guidance on the discharge of mentally disordered people and their continuing care in the community is given in HSG(94)27/LASSL(94)4 and WHC(95)7 and WHC(96)26. The relationship between the CPA, section 117 after-care and local authority arrangements for care management is more fully explained in *Building Bridges - A Guide to arrangements for inter-agency working for the care and protection of severely mentally ill people (Department of Health 1995)*.

27.5 Before the decision is taken to discharge or grant leave to a patient, it is the responsibility of the rmo to ensure, in consultation with the other professionals concerned, that the patient's needs for health and social care are fully assessed and the care plan addresses them. If the patient is being given leave for only a short period a less comprehensive review may suffice but the arrangements for the patient's care should still be properly recorded.

27.6 The rmo is also responsible for ensuring that:

- a proper assessment is made of risks to the patient or other people;

- in the case of offender patients, the circumstances of any victim and their families are taken into account;

- consideration is given to whether the patient meets the criteria for after-care under supervision, or under guardianship (see Chapters 13 and 28); and

- consideration is given to whether the patient should be placed on the supervision register established in accordance with HSG(94)5.

Mental Health Review Tribunals and managers' hearings

27.7 The courts have ruled[16] that in order to fulfil their obligations under section 117 Health Authorities and Local Authority Social Services Authorities must take reasonable steps to identify appropriate after-care facilities for a patient before his or her actual discharge from hospital. In view of this, some discussion of after-care needs, including social services and other relevant professionals and agencies, should take place before a patient has an Mental Health Review Tribunal or managers' hearing, so that suitable after-care arrangements can be implemented in the event of his or her being discharged (see para 22.12).

Who should be involved

27.8 Those who should be involved in consideration of the patient's after-care needs include:

- the patient, if he or she wishes and/or a nominated representative;
- the patient's rmo;
- a nurse involved in caring for the patient in hospital;
- a social worker/care manager specialising in mental health work;
- the GP and primary care team;
- a community psychiatric/mental health nurse;
- a representative of relevant voluntary organisations;
- in the case of a restricted patient, the probation service;
- subject to the patient's consent, any informal carer who will be involved in looking after him or her outside hospital;
- subject to the patient's consent, his or her nearest relative[17];
- a representative of housing authorities, if accommodation is an issue.

27.9 It is important that those who are involved are able to take decisions regarding their own and as far as possible their agency's involvement. If approval for plans needs to be obtained from more senior levels

---

[16] R v Ealing District Health Authority ex parte Fox [1993] 3 All ER 170

[17] There are special considerations governing consultation with the nearest relative of a patient subject to after-care under supervision: see Chapter 28

(for example, for funding) it is important that this causes no delay to the implementation of the care plan.

Considerations for after-care

27.10 Those concerned must consider the following issues:

a. the patient's own wishes and needs, and those of any dependents;

b. the views of any relevant relative, friend or supporter of the patient;

c. the need for agreement with authorities and agencies in the area where the patient is to live;

d. in the case of offender patients, the circumstances of any victim and their families should be taken into account when deciding where the patient should live;

e. the possible involvement of other agencies, eg probation, voluntary organisations;

f. the establishing of a care plan, based on proper assessment and clearly identified needs, including:

   • day time activities or employment

   • appropriate accommodation

   • out-patient treatment

   • counselling, and personal support

   • assistance in welfare rights and managing finances

   • a contingency plan should the patient relapse.

g. the appointment of a key worker (see para 27.2) from either of the statutory agencies to monitor the care plan's implementation, liaise and co-ordinate where necessary and report to the senior officer in their agency any problems that arise which cannot be resolved through discussion;

h. the identification of any unmet need.

27.11 The professionals concerned should establish an agreed outline of the patient's needs, taking into account his or her social and cultural background, and agree a time-scale for the implementation of the various aspects of the plan. All key people with specific responsibilities with regard to the patient should be properly identified. Once plans are agreed it is essential that any changes are discussed with others involved with the patient before being implemented. The plan should be recorded in writing.

27.12 The care plan should be regularly reviewed. It will be the responsibility of the key worker to arrange reviews of the plan until it is agreed that it is no longer necessary. The senior officer in the key worker's agency responsible for after-care arrangements should ensure that all aspects of the procedure are followed.

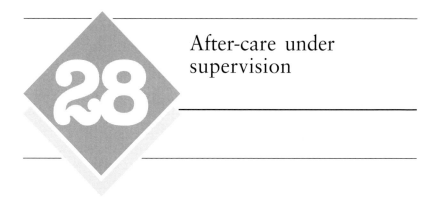

After-care under supervision

(Paras 113-140 of the Memorandum)

28.1 After-care under supervision was introduced in April 1996 by the Mental Health (Patients in the Community) Act 1995. In the introductory guidance, HSG(96)11/LAC(96)8, it is referred to as "supervised discharge".

Purpose

28.2 After-care under supervision is an arrangement by which a patient who has been detained in hospital for treatment under the provisions of the Act may be subject to formal supervision after he or she is discharged. Its purpose is to help ensure that the patient receives the after-care services to be provided under section 117 of the Act. It is available for patients suffering from any of the four forms of mental disorder in the Act but is primarily intended for those with severe mental illness.

Criteria for use of supervision

28.3 The Act may be used to ensure after-care is provided for patients who:

- have been detained for treatment;
- need suitable after-care in respect of their mental disorder to prevent substantial risk of serious harm to themselves or other people, or of serious exploitation.

28.4 Before the patient is discharged, he or she must have a community rmo, who will be responsible for treatment after discharge. The patient must also have an identified supervisor who is a suitably qualified and experienced member of the multi-disciplinary community team. For patients living in England, the supervisor will also fulfil the role of key worker under CPA.

28.5 If a patient needs to receive after-care within a formal structure but he or she does not meet all the criteria for after-care under supervision guardianship under section 7 of the MHA 1983 (see Chapter 13) may be used.

Implementation

28.6 Before the supervision application is made the responsible Health Authority, or the service provider acting for the authority, should meet the responsible Local Authority and seek to agree the arrangements for providing the after-care, including the requirements to be imposed on the patient under the Act. The procedure for this needs to be agreed as part of local liaison arrangements, which should identify the officer who is to act for the local Social Services Authority. The after-care arrangements will have to be drawn up as part of the normal discharge planning process, following the principles of the CPA in England and the Welsh Office Mental Illness Strategy (WHC(95)40) in Wales and in accordance with the formal consultation requirements in the Act.

28.7 The rmo who makes the supervision application is responsible for consulting both the current and the proposed future care team about the arrangements for after-care and the requirements to be imposed. The rmo should ensure that agreement about a care plan is reached between all involved. Details of the after-care to be provided must be attached to the supervision application and the rmo must list the requirements to be imposed and name the supervisor and rmo.

Admission to hospital

28.8 After-care under supervision will end completely if the patient is admitted to hospital under section 3 or 37 of the Act. If the patient is admitted to hospital under section 2, or informally, the after-care will merely be suspended: the patient temporarily ceases to receive after-care and have requirements imposed. The period of after-care under supervision will continue to run whilst the patient is in hospital and if it does not expire it will continue after discharge for the remainder of the period, if any. In the case of an informal patient, if the period of after-care under supervision would expire before the expected date of discharge, the need for renewal should be considered in the normal way and any necessary action taken. In the case of a patient admitted under section 2, if the period expires before discharge it will be deemed to be extended for 28 days after discharge for the purpose of renewal. The same will apply if the period of after-care under supervision has up to 28 days to run after the discharge of a patient detained under section 2.

Further guidance

28.9 Further guidance on after-care under supervision can be found in *Guidance on Supervised Discharge (After-care under Supervision) and Related Provisions* which was published under HSG(96)11/LAC(96)8 and WHC(96)11 and which remains extant.

Part III of the Act - patients concerned with criminal proceedings

Discharge and supervision

29.1 Those involved in the supervision of a conditionally discharged restricted patient should have copies of and be familiar with *Supervision and After-Care of Conditionally Discharged Restricted Patients* (HO/DHSS notes of guidance 1987 and the guidance for social supervisors in this series updated in 1997) and *Recall of Mentally Disordered Patients subject to restrictions on discharge* (HSG(93)20/LAC(93)9).

Recall

29.2 If a conditionally discharged restricted patient requires hospital admission, it will not always be necessary for the Home Secretary to recall the patient to hospital. For example,

a. The patient may be willing to accept treatment informally. In these circumstances, however, care should be taken to ensure that the patient's consent is freely given, if he or she is capable of giving consent. If the patient is incapable of giving consent, it is advisable to consider whether treatment may be given under the common law doctrine of necessity or whether the Home Secretary should recall the patient.

b. In some cases it may be appropriate to consider admitting the patient under Part II of the Act as an alternative[18].

c. It may not always be necessary to recall the patient to the same hospital from which he or she was conditionally discharged. In some

---

[18] R v North West London Mental Health Trust ex parte Stewart [1998]

cases recall to hospital with a lesser, or greater, degree of security will be appropriate.

29.3 When a recall is being considered this should be discussed between the doctor, the social supervisor and the Mental Health Unit of the Home Office.

29.4 When a patient is recalled, the person taking him or her into custody should explain that the patient is being recalled to hospital by the Home Secretary and will be given a fuller explanation later. As soon as possible after admission to hospital, and in any event within 72 hours of admission, the rmo or deputy, and an ASW or a representative of the hospital management, should explain to the patient the reason for the recall and ensure, in so far as the patient's mental state allows, that he or she understands. The patient should also be informed that his or her case will be referred to a Mental Health Review Tribunal within one month.

29.5 The patient's rmo should ensure that:

- the patient is given assistance to inform his or her legal adviser (if any);
- subject to the patient's consent, his or her nearest relative and/or other relative or friend is told.

Return to court

29.6 All professionals concerned with ensuring the return to court of a patient on remand or under an interim hospital order should be familiar with the contents of paras 31-33 of Home Office circular number 71/1984 on the implementation of sections 35, 36, 38 and 40(3) of the Mental Health Act. When a patient has been admitted on remand or subject to an interim hospital order, it is the responsibility of the hospital to return the patient to court as required. The court should give adequate notice of the hearing. The hospital should liaise with the courts in plenty of time to confirm the arrangements for escorting the patient to and from hospital. The hospital will be responsible for providing a suitable escort for the patient when travelling from the hospital to the court and should plan for the provision of necessary staff to do this. The assistance of the police may be requested if necessary. Once on the court premises, the patient will come under the supervision of the police or prison officers there.

People with learning disabilities

General

30.1 The guidance given elsewhere in the Code applies to patients with learning disabilities. This chapter gives guidance on a number of particular issues of importance to this group of patients.

30.2 Very few people with learning disabilities are detained under the Act. Where people with learning disabilities fall within the legal definition of mental disorder they may be considered for admission under section 2 and detention under sections 5, 135 and 136. Other admission sections can only be considered if the person falls within the legal definition of mental impairment or severe mental impairment. But admission of a person with learning disability for treatment under the Act may also be considered if he or she also suffers from another form of mental disorder (for example mental illness).

Communication

30.3 The assessment of a person with learning disabilities requires special consideration to enable communication with the person being assessed. Where possible the ASW should have had experience of working with people with learning disabilities or be able to call upon someone who has. It is important that someone who knows the patient and can communicate with him or her is present at the assessment. The ASW should seek assistance from the community team for learning disabilities.

Assessment

30.4 No patient should be classified under the Act as mentally impaired or severely mentally impaired without an assessment by a consultant psychiatrist in learning disabilities and a formal psychological assessment. This assessment should be part of a complete appraisal by medical, nursing, social work and psychology professionals with experience in learning disabilities, in consultation with a relative, friend or supporter of the patient. Contact with the specialist hospital units for deafness and mental health may help to forestall deaf people being wrongly assessed as learning disabled. These procedures should also be followed, except in emergencies, where it is proposed that a patient is to be admitted under section 2 on the grounds of mental disorder.

Mental impairment/severe mental impairment (legally defined in section 1)

30.5 The identification of an individual who falls within these legal categories is a matter for clinical judgement, guided by current professional practice and subject to the relevant legal requirements. Those assessing the patient must be satisfied that he or she displays a number of characteristics; these are difficult to define in practice. The following is general guidance in relation to the key factors or components of these legal categories.

Incomplete or arrested development of mind. This implies that the features that determine the learning disability were present at some stage which permanently prevented the usual maturation of intellectual and social development. It excludes persons whose learning disability derives from accident, injury or illness occurring after that point usually accepted as complete development.

Severe or significant impairment of intelligence. The judgment as to the presence of this particular characteristic must be made on the basis of reliable and careful assessment.

Severe or significant impairment of social functioning. The evidence of the degree and nature of social competence should be based on reliable and recent observations, preferably from a number of sources such as social workers, nurses and psychologists. Such evidence should include the results of one or more social functioning assessment tests.

Abnormally aggressive behaviour. Any assessment of this category should be based on observations of behaviour which lead to a conclusion that the actions are outside the usual range of aggressive behaviour, and which cause actual damage and/or real distress occurring recently or persistently or with excessive severity.

Irresponsible conduct. The assessment of this characteristic should be based on an observation of behaviour which shows a lack of responsibility, a disregard of the consequences of action taken, and where the results cause actual damage or real distress, either recently or persistently or with excessive severity.

30.6 A person who has severe learning disabilities and lacks the capacity to make personal health care decisions may be admitted to hospital on an informal basis if he or she does not object to being an in-patient. In that case the patient's admission and care must in his or her best interests and in accordance with the common law doctrine of necessity (see paras 2.8 and 15.21).

Children and young people under the age of 18

Introduction

31.1 The Code of Practice applies to all patients including children and young people under the age of 18 (referred to in this Chapter as children). This Chapter gives guidance on a number of issues of particular importance affecting children. There is no minimum age limit for admission to hospital under the Act (but only a person who has attained the age of 16 can be subject to guardianship or after-care under supervision).

The legal framework and legal advice

31.2 The legal framework governing the admission to hospital and treatment of children is complex. It is the responsibility of all professionals, local social services authorities and education authorities and Trusts to ensure that necessary information (including the Code of Practice, the Act, the Children Act and in particular volumes 1, 4, 6 and 7 of the Children Act Guidance) is available to all those responsible for the care of children.

31.3 Where it is considered necessary to require a child's residence in a particular place and/or to require them to undergo medical treatment the choice between the Act and the Children Act is not always easy. When considering which provisions to use it is particularly important to identify the primary purpose of the proposed intervention. For example, a seriously mentally ill child may require treatment under the Act, whereas the needs of a behaviourally disturbed child may be more appropriately met within secure accommodation under the Children Act. Professional staff who address these questions should:

a. be aware of the relevant statutory provisions and have easy access to competent legal advice;

b. keep in mind the importance of ensuring that the child's care and treatment is managed with clarity, consistency and within a recognisable framework; and

c. attempt to select the option that reflects the predominant needs of the child at that time whether that be to provide specific mental health care and treatment or to achieve a measure of safety and protection. Either way the least restrictive option consistent with the care and treatment objectives for the child should be sought.

Guiding principles

31.4 The guidance set out in Chapter 1 applies equally to children although in the case of children there will be special considerations. In particular:

a. children should be kept as fully informed as possible about their care and treatment, and their views and wishes ascertained and taken into account, having regard to their age and understanding. It is important to remember, including in the case of older children, that the impact of the child's wishes on the parents or other person with parental responsibility should always be considered;

b. any intervention in the life of a child considered necessary by reason of their mental disorder, should be the least restrictive possible and result in the least possible segregation from family, friends, community and school; and

c. all children in hospital should receive appropriate education (see joint DH/DFEE guidance - The Education of Sick Children, DFEE Circular number 12/94, DH circulars LAC(94)10 and HSG (94)24, May 1994).

31.5 Whenever the care and treatment of a child under the age of 16 is being considered, the following questions (amongst many others) need to be asked. It may also be appropriate to ask the following questions in the case of the older child:

a. Who has parental responsibility for the child? It is essential that those responsible for the care and treatment of the child always request copies of any court orders for reference on the hospital ward. These orders may include care orders, residence orders, contact orders, evidence of appointment as the child's guardian, parental responsibility agreements or orders under section 4 of the Children Act and any order under wardship;

b. If the child is living with either of the parents who are separated, whether there is a residence order and if so in whose favour. It may be necessary to consider whether it is appropriate to contact both parents;

c. What is the capacity of the child to make his or her own decisions in terms of emotional maturity, intellectual capacity and mental state? (see Chapter 15 and paragraph 31.11);

d. Where a parent or other person with parental responsibility refuses consent to treatment, how sound are the reasons and on what grounds are they made?; and

e. Could the needs of the child be met in a social services or educational placement? To what extent have these authorities carefully considered all possible alternative suitable placements?

Informal admission to hospital

Children under 16

31.6 The parents or other person with parental responsibility may arrange for the admission of children under the age of 16 to hospital as informal patients. Where a doctor concludes that such a child has the capacity to make such a decision for him or herself (i.e. he or she is of sufficient intelligence and understanding to make that decision - that is to say "Gillick competent", see paragraph 31.11) and the child objects to such admission then the consent of the person with parental responsibility may be sufficient authority to enable the child to be admitted against their wishes. Where a "Gillick competent" child wishes to discharge him or herself as an informal patient from hospital, the contrary wishes of any person who has parental responsibility will ordinarily prevail. In either circumstance consideration should be given to whether the use of the Act, if applicable, would be appropriate (see also paragraph 31.13).

31.7 Where a "Gillick competent" child is willing to be admitted but the parents or other person with parental responsibility object, their views should be seriously considered and given due weight but their objections to such admission will not prevail.

16 or 17 year olds

31.8 Section 131(2) of the Act provides that any 16 and 17 year old "capable of expressing his own wishes" can admit him or herself as an informal patient to hospital, irrespective of the wishes of his or her parent or guardian. Where a 16 or 17 year old is unwilling to remain in hospital as an informal patient, consideration may need to be given to whether he or she should be detained under the Act.

31.9 Where a 16 or 17 year old is incapable of expressing his own wishes, the consent of the parents should be obtained or consideration given to the use of the Act.

Consent to medical treatment (see Chapters 15 and 16)

31.10 It is normal practice in relation to the treatment of a child to obtain the consent of the parent (or other person with parental responsibility) as an exercise of their parental responsibility. There are circumstances, however, in which the child will decide for him or herself.

Children under the age of 16

31.11 A "Gillick competent" child can give a valid consent to medical treatment. A child may be regarded as "Gillick competent" if the doctor concludes that he or she has the capacity to make the decision to have the proposed treatment and is of sufficient understanding and intelligence to be capable of making up his/her own mind[19].

---

[19] Gillick v West Norfolk and Wisbech Area Health Authority and Another [1986] AC 112. Capacity is dealt with in Chapter 15, paragraph 15.9 et seq. although it is important in assessing whether a child is to be regarded as "Gillick competent" to have regard to the decision of the Court of Appeal in Re R [1992] 1FLR 190. In that case the Court of Appeal stated that ""Gillick - competence" is a developmental concept and will not be lost or acquired on a day to day or week to week basis. In the case of mental disability, that disability must also be taken into account, particularly where it is fluctuating in its effect."

31.12 The refusal of a "Gillick competent" child to be medically treated can be overridden by the courts or by their parents [20].

31.13 The assistance of the court may be sought, in particular in the following circumstances:

- in the case of a child who is not 16 or "Gillick competent" where treatment decisions need to be made and the person with parental responsibility cannot be identified or is incapacitated, for example in dealing with a child who is accommodated by a local authority;
- where a person with parental responsibility may not be acting in the best interests of the child in making treatment decisions on behalf of the child.

A child's refusal to be treated is a very important consideration in making clinical judgements and for parents and the court in deciding whether themselves to give consent. Its importance increases with age and maturity of the child.

31.14 In cases involving emergency protection orders, child assessment orders, interim care orders and full supervision orders, the Children Act specifically provides that a child may refuse assessment, examination or treatment. (See respectively Children Act section 44(8), section 43(8), section 38(6) and section 35 and Schedule 3 Part I paragraph 4(4).) However, the inherent jurisdiction of the High Court can be used to override a child's refusal, where it considers it should do so[21].

16 and 17 year olds

31.15 Section 8(1) of the Family Law Reform Act 1969 provides that a child of 16 years or over may consent "to any surgical, medical or dental treatment which, in the absence of consent, would constitute a trespass to his person, [and the consent] shall be as effective as it would be if he were of full age; and where a minor has by virtue of this section given an effective consent to any treatment, it shall not be necessary to obtain any consent for it from his parent or guardian."

---

[20] Re W [1992] 4 All ER 627
[21] South Glamorgan CC v W & B [1993] 1 FLR 57

31.16 Where a 16 or 17 year old is regarded as incapable of consenting to treatment the consent of the parents or other person with parental responsibility should be obtained. The refusal of a competent 16 or 17 year old to be medically treated can be overridden by their parents or other person who has parental responsibility for that 16 or 17 year old or by the court. Consideration should be given to whether the use of the Act, if applicable, would be appropriate.

Emergency treatment

31.17 In an emergency situation a doctor may undertake treatment if delay would be dangerous (see para 15.25). It is good practice in that situation to attempt to obtain the consent of the parents or other person with parental responsibility.

Children looked after by the local authority

31.18 Where children are looked after by the local authority (see section 20 of the Children Act), treatment decisions should usually be discussed with the parent or other person with parental responsibility. If a child is voluntarily accommodated by the local authority, the consent of the parent or other person with parental responsibility to the proposed treatment should be obtained. If the child is subject to a care order, the parents share parental responsibility with the local authority and it will be a matter for agreement/negotiation between them as to who should be consulted although it should be remembered that local authorities can, in the exercise of their powers under section 33(3)(b) of the Children Act limit the extent to which parents may exercise their parental responsibility.

Parents/guardians consent

31.19 The fact that a child has been informally admitted by parents or other person with parental responsibility should not lead professionals to assume that they have consented to all components of a treatment programme regarded as "necessary". Consent should be sought for each aspect of the child's care and treatment as it arises. "Blanket" consent forms should not be used.

Information

31.20 The advice concerning the giving of information (see Chapter 14) applies with equal force to children. In particular where such patients are detained under the Act, it is important that assistance is given to enable their legal representation at any Mental Health Review Tribunal.

Confidentiality

31.21 Children's rights to confidentiality should be strictly observed. It is important that all professionals have a clear understanding of their obligations of confidentiality to children and that any limits to such an obligation are made clear to a child who has the capacity to understand them (see paragraphs 4.10 and 4.11 of the DH Guidance on confidentiality *The Protection and Use of Patient Information, Department of Health, March 1996*, HSG(96)18).

Placement

31.22 It is usually preferable for children admitted to hospital to be accommodated with others of their own age group in children's wards or adolescent units, separate from adults. If, exceptionally, this is not practicable, discrete accommodation in an adult ward, with facilities, security and staffing appropriate to the needs of the child might provide the most satisfactory solution.

Complaints

31.23 See Chapter 24.

Welfare of certain hospital patients

31.24 Local authorities should ensure that they arrange for visits to be made to:

- children looked after by them whether or not under a care order who are in hospital, and
- those accommodated or intended to be accommodated for 3 months or more by Health Authorities, Trusts, local education authorities or in residential care, nursing or mental nursing homes (see Review of Children's Cases Regulations 1991 S.I.1991/895 as amended and

sections 85 and 86 of the Children Act). This is in addition to their duty in respect to children in their care in hospitals or nursing homes in England and Wales as required by section 116 of the Act. Local authorities should take such other steps in relation to the patient while in hospital or nursing home as would be expected to be taken by his or her parent. Local authorities are under a duty to:

- promote contact between children who are in need and their families if they live away from home and to help them get back together (paragraphs 10 and 15 of Schedule 2 to the Children Act); and

- to arrange for persons (independent visitors) to visit and befriend children looked after by the authority wherever they are if they have not been regularly visited by their parents (paragraph 17 of Schedule 2 to the Act).

Annex A

	TITLE	PUBLICATION DATE
Practice Note 1	Guidance on Administration of Clozapine and Other Treatments Requiring Blood Tests under the Provisions of Part IV of the Mental Health Act	June 1993
Practice Note 2	Nurses, the Administration of Medicine for Mental Disorder and the Mental Health Act	March 1994
Practice Note 3	Section 5(2) of the 1983 Mental Health Act and Transfers	March 1994
Practice Note 4	Section 17 of the Mental Health Act 1983	May 1996
Practice Note 5	Guidance on Issues Relating to the Administration of the Mental Health Act in Mental Nursing Homes Registered to Receive Detained Patients	July 1996

Guidance Note 1	Guidance to Health Authorities: the Mental Health Act 1983	December 1996
Guidance Note 2	GPs and the Mental Health Act	December 1996
Guidance Note 3	Guidance on the Treatment of Anorexia Nervosa under the Mental Health Act 1983	August 1997
Position Paper 1	Research and Detained Patients	January 1997
Discussion Paper 1	The Threshold for Admission and the Deteriorating Patient	June 1998

Annex B

Case name and Law Report Reference (where available)	Subject	Paragraph
B v Croydon Health Authority [1995] 2 WLR 294	Medical treatment of symptoms of mental disorder (naso-gastric feeding)	16.5
R v Managers of Warley Hospital ex parte Barker [1998] COD 309	Renewal of detention while patient on leave of absence	20.10 20.13
Gillick v West Norfolk and Wisbech Area Health Authority [1986] AC 112	When child under 16 has capacity to consent to treatment without consent of parent	31.11
R v Bournewood Community and Mental Health NHS Trust ex parte L [1998] All ER 319	Informal admission and treatment of mentally incapacitated patients	2.8 8.4 15.21 30.6
R v Broadmoor Special Hospital Authority ex parte S [1998] COD 199	Power to search patients detained under the Act	25.3

Case name and Law Report Reference (where available)	Subject	Paragraph
R v Collins ex parte S (no 2) [1998]	Refusal to consent to invasive treatment (Guidelines)	15.11
R v Ealing District Health Authority ex parte Fox [1993] 3 All ER 170	Duty to provide section 117 after-care services	22.12 27.7
R v North West London Mental Health Trust ex parte Stewart [1998]	Part II admission of conditionally discharged patient	29.2 b.
R v Riverside Mental Health NHS Trust ex parte Huzzey [1998]	Discharge by managers after nearest relative's discharge barred	23.12
R v Wilson ex parte W [1996] COD 42	No successive section 2 applications	5.5
Re C [1994] 1 FLR 31	Capacity to decide on leg amputation	15.10
Re F [1990] 2 AC 1	Treatment of mentally incapacitated patient: doctrine of necessity	15.21
Re MB [1997] 2 FCR 541	Test of capacity to consent to invasive treatment	15.10
Re R [1992] 1 FLR 190	Fluctuating mental disorder and Gillick competency	31.10

Case name and Law Report Reference (where available)	Subject	Paragraph
Re W [1992] 4 All ER 627	Refusal of treatment by Gillick competent child	31.12

Index

AFTER-CARE UNDER SUPERVISION:

- admission to hospital 28.8
- criteria for use of supervision 28.3–28.5
- further guidance 28.9
- purpose 28.2

APPROVED DOCTORS:

- Health Authority responsibility for approving 2.40–2.42

APPROVED SOCIAL WORKERS:

- displacement of nearest relative 2.18
- as applicant for admission 2.35–2.36
- decision not to apply for admission 2.31–2.32
- responsibilities for Mentally Disordered Offenders to be admitted 3.19
- responsibilities in assessment process 2.11–2.21
- when considering emergency admissions 6.5
- responsibilities in relation to conveying to hospital 11.3

ASSESSMENT:

- criminal proceedings 3.1–3.10
- disagreements between professionals 2.33–2.34
- factors to be taken into account 2.6
- for guardianship 13.3–13.4
- health of patient 2.10
- individual professional responsibilities 2.11–2.30
- mentally disordered person found in public places 10.12–10.15
- people with learning disabilities 30.4
- prior to admission 2.5
- protection of others 2.9
- request from nearest relative to assess 2.35

AUTHORITIES: *see also under local and health*

- joint responsibilities 2.39

BEHAVIOUR MODIFICATION: *see Psychological Treatments*

CARE PLAN:

- for after-care 27.9–27.12

CHILDREN AND YOUNG PEOPLE:

- admission 31.6–31.9
- complaints 31.23
- confidentiality 31.21
- consent to medical treatment 31.10–31.19
- in care 31.18
- in secure accommodation 31.18
- information 31.20
- legal framework 31.2–31.3
- M H R Ts/access to 31.20
- placement 31.22
- practice principles 31.4–31.5
- welfare of certain people in hospital 31.24

COMPLAINTS:

- children and young people 31.23
- Hospital Complaints Procedure Act 24.1
- managers' duties 24.2
- publicity 14.2
- recording 24.3
- staff responsibilities 24.2
- confidentiality 1.8

CONSENT TO TREATMENT:

- basic principles 15.13
- capacity to give consent 15.8–15.12 & 15.14–15.17
- incapacity to give consent 15.18–15.25
- information on 14.5a
- medication 16.11–16.18
- mentally disordered persons found in public places 10.16

INFORMATION:

- children and young people 31.20
- communicating with patients 1.3–1.7
- display of information 1.12
- Managers' duties 1.10–1.11 & 14.1–14.3
- particular information 14.5
- patients with sensory impairment 1.4
- recording 14.4d
- statutory information 1.12 & 14.5
- who should give information 14.4c

INTERPRETERS:

- access to 1.4

LEAVE OF ABSENCE:

- duration and renewal 20.13
- general principles 20.1–20.2
- medical treatment 20.8
- power to grant 20.3
- recall to hospital 20.11–20.12
- recording and information 20.6
- revoking 20.11

LOCAL AUTHORITIES:

- duties in relation to guardianship 13.7
- policy on patients absent without leave 21.5–21.6
- responsibilities in relation to admission 2.37–2.38
- responsibilities in relation to doctor's holding power 8.1b
- responsibilities for establishing aftercare arrangements 27.3
- powers of entry 10.19

LOCKED DOORS ON OPEN WARDS:

- general principles 19.24–19.27
- under nurse's holding power 9.9

- review of detention 23.2–23.20
- roles and responsibilities in relation to S O A Ds 16.23
- transfer 22.9

MEDICAL EXAMINATION:

- requirements for 2.23

MEDICAL PRACTITIONERS:

- approval under section 12 2.40–2.42

MEDICAL RECOMMENDATION:

- joint 2.27
- private practice 4.1–4.5
- second medical recommendation 2.29–2.30

MEDICAL TREATMENT:

- children and young people 31.10–31.19
- common law 15.8
- compliance with part IV of the Act 16.2–16.3
- consent not given 15.25
- consent to treatment 15.13–15.17
- definition of 15.4
- duty of r m o 15.2
- incapacity to give consent 15.18–15.24
- interpretation 15.4
- leave of absence 20.8
- managers' role 15.3
- mentally disordered persons found in public places 10.16
- medication 16.11–16.18
- part IV provisions 16.2–16.5 & 16.42–16.44
- psychosurgery 16.7
- review of treatment 16.35–16.37
- sterilisation 15.22–15.24
- surgical implantation of hormones 16.7–16.8
- treatment not requiring consent under the Act 16.38–16.39

PART II SECTIONS

- choice 5.4–5.5
- section 2 5.2
- section 3 5.3

PATIENTS ABSENT WITHOUT LEAVE: 21.1–21.4

PEOPLE WITH LEARNING DISABILITIES

- assessment 30.4
- communication 30.3
- general 30.1–30.2
- mental impairment/severe mental impairment 30.5–30.6

PERSONAL SEARCHES: 25.1–25.9

POLICE POWER TO REMOVE TO A PLACE OF SAFETY:

- assessment 10.12–10.15
- compulsory admission 10.18
- good practice 10.1–10.6
- information about rights 10.9–10.11
- place of safety 10.5
- record keeping 10.7–10.8
- the power 10.19
- treatment 10.16

PRIVATE PRACTICE:

- medical recommendations 4.1–4.5

PROFESSIONAL RESPONSIBILITY:

- criminal proceedings 3.3

PSYCHOLOGICAL TREATMENTS:

- basic principles 18.1
- behaviour modification programmes 19.2–19.8
- time out 19.9–19.10

VICTIMS:

VISITING:

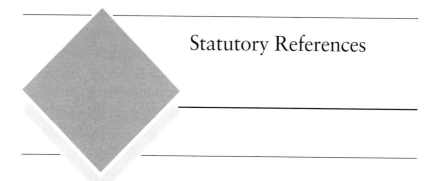

Statutory References

Children Act 1989

31.2–31.4

Section
4	31.5
20	31.18
33	31.18
35	31.14
38	31.14
43	31.14
44	31.14
85	31.24
86	31.24

Crime & Disorder Act 1998

Section
115	1.8

Crime (Sentences) Act 1997

5.15

Criminal Justice Act 1991

Section
4	3.12
39A	3.5

Hospital Complaints & Procedures Act 1985

24.3

Family Law Reform Act 1969

Section
8	31.15

Mental Heath Act 1983

Section
1	2.22, 3.16, 30.5
2	2.9, 2.10, 2.15, 2.31,3.19, ch5, 6.4, 6.7, 8.3, 8.9, 8.12, 10.18, 13.9, 28.8, 30.2, 30.4
3	2.6, 2.9, 2.10, 2.16, 2.31, 3.19, ch5, 8.3, 8.9, 8.12, 10.18, 13.9, 17.3, 22.16, 28.8
4	ch6, 8.9, 10.18, 13.9, 16.2
5	ch8, ch9, 10.7, 10.18, 16.2, 16.12, 30.2

Mental Health Act 1983 cont.

Section

7	ch13, 28.5
8	13.8, 31.15
11	2.14–2.16
12	2.40, 2.42, 4.1, 10.12, 20.3
13	2.31, 2.32, 2.35, 2.38, 10.16, 10.18
15	12.3
17	16.1, ch20, 27.3
18	ch21
19	8.17, 20.1, 20.10, 22.9, 22.16
20	23.7, 23.15, 23.20
23	2.16, 20.10, ch23
25	13.2, 23.8, 23.12
26	1.10, 2.14
29	2.18, 5.5
35	7.3, 16.2, 16.12, ch17, 20.1, 29.6, 31.14
36	7.8, 17.1, 20.1, 29.6
37	3.16, 7.3, 13.11, 16.2, 16.12, 28.8
38	3.10, 7.8, 20.1, 29.6, 31.14
39	3.4, 3.5
40	29.6
42	16.2
43	31.14
44	31.14
45	3.16
47	3.16, 7.2
48	7.2
49	3.16
57	16.2, 16.6–16.8, 16.36, 16.38
58	ch16
61	16.23, 16.27, 16.35–37
62	16.2, 16.16, 16.19, 16.27, 16.40–16.42
63	16.2, 16.38, 16.39
66	5.3
68	22.16
73	16.2
74	16.2
116	31.24
117	20.7, 22.12, 27.3, 27.4, 27.7, 28.2
129	13.8
131	31.8
132	8.7, 10.10, 10.11, 13.7, 14.1, 22.13
133	14.3, 22.13
134	22.14, 22.15, 26.5
135	2.12, 2.24, 30.2
136	ch10, 16.2, 16.12, 30.2
145	16.38

Mental Health (Hospital, Guardianship & Consent to Treatment) Regulations 1983

Section

19	13.9

Mental Health (Patients in the Community) Act 1995

28.1

Nurses, Midwives and Health Visitors Act 1997

9.1

Police and Criminal Evidence Act 1984

Glossary

Act, the	Mental Health Act 1983
After-care under supervision (supervised discharge)	Defined in s 25A
Applicant, the	The patient's nearest relative or an Approved Social Worker (S 11)
Approved Social Worker (ASW)	Defined in s 145(1) (but see S114)
Community Psychiatric Nurse (CPN)	First reference 2.16
Community Responsible Medical Officer (crmo)	Defined in S 34(1)
Forms	Details of the forms referred to in the Code of Practice can be found in schedule 1 of The Mental Health (Hospital, Guardianship and Consent to Treatment) Regulations 1983 (SI 1983 No 893 as amended by SI 1996 No 540 and SI 1998 No 2624)
Hospital	Defined in S 145(1)
Local social services authority	Defined in S 145(1)
Managers, the	Defined in S 145(1)
Memorandum, the	Explanatory Memorandum on Parts I to VI, VIII and X of the Mental Health Act 1983. Department of Health (TSO 1998)

Medical Treatment	See S 145(1)
Mental Disorder (and sub categories of mental disorder)	Defined in S 1
Mental Nursing Home	Defined in S 145(1)
Nearest Relative	Defined in S 26
Nominated Medical Attendant	Defined in S 34(1)
Patient	Defined in S 145(1)
Place of Safety	Defined in S 135(6) (and s55(1) for Part III of the Act)
Regulations	There are a number of regulations, orders made under the Act. The most important, for the purposes of understanding this Code are The Mental Health (Hospital, Guardianship and Consent to Treatment) Regulations 1983 (SI 1983 No 893 as amended by SI 1996 No 540 and SI 1998 No 2624)
Responsible Medical Officer (rmo)	Defined in S 34(1)
Second Opinion Appointed Doctor (SOAD)	Doctors appointed by the Mental Health Act Commission to provide second opinions on treatment under Part VI of the Act

Printed in the United Kingdom for The Stationery Office
J100430 12/99 C50 9385 11830

DK findout!

Stone Age

Author: Klint Janulis
Consultant: James Dilley

DK | Penguin
Random
House

Senior editor Marie Greenwood
Project art editor Joanne Clark
Editor Caryn Jenner
Design assistant Rhea Gaughan
Editorial assistant Kathleen Teece
Additional design Emma Hobson
Jacket design Amy Keast
Jacket co-ordinator Francesca Young
Managing editor Laura Gilbert
Managing art editor Diane Peyton Jones
Pre-production producer Dragana Puvacic
Producer Srijana Gurung
Art director Martin Wilson
Publisher Sarah Larter
Publishing director Sophie Mitchell
Educational consultant Jacqueline Harris

First published in Great Britain in 2017 by
Dorling Kindersley Limited
One Embassy Gardens, 8 Viaduct Gardens, London, SW11 7BW

Copyright © 2017 Dorling Kindersley Limited
A Penguin Random House Company
10 9
014–298640–January/2017

All rights reserved.
No part of this publication may be reproduced, stored in
or introduced into a retrieval system, or transmitted, in
any form, or by any means (electronic, mechanical,
photocopying, recording, or otherwise), without the
prior written permission of the copyright owner.

A CIP catalogue record for this book
is available from the British Library.
ISBN: 978-0-2412-8270-0

Printed and bound in China

A WORLD OF IDEAS:
SEE ALL THERE IS TO KNOW

www.dk.com

BCE/CE
When you see the letters BCE, it means Before
the Common Era, which began in the year
1 CE (Common Era).

Contents

Mammoth

Handaxe

2

Carved spear-thrower tip

Shaman

Neanderthal skull

Hunter with spear

Bone necklace

3

What is the Stone Age?

The Stone Age covers almost all of human history. It was the time when humans used stone tools. Through most of the Stone Age, people were hunter-gatherers. They looked for food by hunting, fishing, and collecting plants and fruit to eat. Gradually, early people developed to live in groups and communicate with each other, much like we do today. The Stone Age can be divided into three main periods, as shown here.

Old Stone Age (Paleolithic)

This is the biggest Stone Age time period as it covers more than 3 million years of human history. It is the time when people started to develop, or evolve, in many important ways, such as by making simple stone tools.

Flint handaxe

Harpoon tips

How people developed

Our ancestors learned to make stone tools and this allowed them to get food much more easily. Over many generations, this resulted in humans becoming cleverer and better at tool-making, with larger brains and different bodies, eventually becoming the species we are today, *Homo sapiens*.

The shape and size of the skulls of early humans changed over time.

Early human
Living in Africa, Europe, and Asia between 600,000 and 200,000 years ago, *Homo heidelbergensis* is the direct ancestor of humans and Neanderthals. They could hunt, make complex stone tools, and use fire.

Old Stone age
3.3.million years ago–11,500 years ago

Middle Stone Age
11,500–6,500 years ago

New Stone Age
6,500–4,000 years ago

After the Stone Age
4,000 years ago

Neolithic polished axe head

New Stone Age (Neolithic)

"Neo" means "new", and it describes a time when people moved away from hunting and gathering, and became farmers in many parts of the world. However, people still continued to use stone tools.

Microliths (blade points)

Bronze Age axe

After the Stone Age

Some societies started to make metal tools during periods called the Bronze Age and Iron Age. However, to this day there are still people in the world living as hunter-gatherers.

Middle Stone Age (Mesolithic)

During this time, icy glaciers were melting and the seas were rising. People developed the tools they needed to deal with these changes. They became better at certain hunting skills, such as using harpoons (long spears) for catching fish.

Sickle for cutting grain

Iron Age helmet

Neanderthals had bigger eyes and brains than humans.

Homo sapiens had smaller brains than Neanderthals.

Neanderthal
Neanderthals (*Homo neanderthalensis*) are our closest relatives. They lived between 250,000 and about 24,000 years ago. They had bigger brains than humans and it is not understood exactly why they died out.

Homo sapien
Humans that looked like we do today appeared in Africa about 200,000 years ago, but we are not sure how similar their brains were to ours today. About 12,000 years ago, they had spread to most of the world.

Stone Age hunter

Stone Age hunters like this one lived towards the end of the Stone Age. They used animal skins to keep warm and to build shelters. They were skilled at making stone tools, rope and, fire. They were strong and capable, and true adventurers!

» **Species:** *Homo Sapiens*

» **Time period:** Late Stone Age

» **Where did they live:** Every continent apart from Antarctica

Meet a Stone Age human

Stone Age people had the same basic needs that people do today. We all need food, clothing, shelter, and companionship. But Stone Age people had to go out and hunt for their own food. They made their own clothes and shelters. In some ways, they were more skilful than we are today! Let's compare a Stone Age hunter with a modern adventurer ...

Animal-skin shelter
When following herds of animals, people needed shelters that were quick and light to put up, like this one made from deer skin.

Stone Age human wears a tunic made from animal skin for protection from the cold.

Cordage
Cordage was rope made from plant or animal fibres. It was used for everything, including carrying firewood, making baskets, and building shelters.

Fire-making kit
Making fire was an essential skill. One way was to use a bow and a stick (drill) to create fire by friction. This was called the bow-drill method.

Stone tools
Stone tools helped people to cut down branches, hunt, and prepare food. Making stone tools was one of the first skills humans mastered, and was essential for their survival.

Bull roarer
This was a piece of wood or bone attached to rope that made a loud noise when spun around. It was a way of checking to see if other people were nearby.

Tent
Nylon tents used by campers today are lighter than Stone Age shelters. Instead of branches for the frame, they have thin aluminium poles that can be reused.

Today's human wears a waterproof jacket for protection from wind and rain

Rope
Campers use lightweight but strong nylon rope. It is similar to cordage, but even stronger.

Matches
Modern-day adventurers use matches, lighters, and fire starters to make fire out in the wilderness.

Knife
A multi-tool or Swiss Army knife can do many of the same things a stone tool can do, like cut, shave, pierce, or saw materials.

Mobile phone
Where would we be without our mobile phones? Today, people use their phones to communicate instantly with each other from afar.

FACT FILE

Modern day adventurer

Modern humans do not need to hunt animals for food and skins to survive. They can go to a shop to buy the food and equipment they need. The tools they use have been designed and made by specialists. Are they real adventurers?

» **Species:** *Homo Sapiens*

» **Time period:** Present day

» **Where do they live:** Every continent including Antarctica

Otzi the Iceman

The fully dressed body of Stone Age adventurer Otzi the Iceman was found in a glacier in the Austrian Alps. He was wearing a bearskin hat and had a waterproof cloak made of grass. Studies on his body showed that Otzi had been murdered by being struck with an arrow and then being hit on the head.

Stone Age arrowheads

! WOW!

Tattooing goes back to the Stone Age! Otzi had over **60 tattoos** on his body!

Where did they live?

Early in the Stone Age, the first people spread out from Africa to Europe and Asia. Eventually, over thousands of years, early people travelled across the world. They adapted to different environments, from the freezing Arctic to the hot, dry climate of Australia.

Settlers in Greenland hunted sea birds.

1 Greenland

People who settled in Greenland learned to hunt and find food in freezing ocean waters. They made boats and special tools for hunting in the ocean. Even today, some people still follow some of the same traditions.

GREENLAND
1

NORTH AMERICA

3
EUROPE

AFRIC

SOUTH AMERICA
2

People in South America hunted llama and deer with stone tools.

2 Americas

North and South America are known as the Americas. These were the last areas to be settled. People spread across both continents, some living as hunter-gatherers, others as farmers.

People in Stone Age Europe hunted, fished, and gathered fruit and nuts.

3 Europe

People arrived in mainland Europe about 40,000 years ago. They reached the British Isles much later – near the end of the last Ice Age, around 10,000 years ago. These early Europeans had to cope with icy glaciers and very cold weather.

4 Africa

The first humans developed in Africa, where they began to walk on two legs and use stone tools. Some of these early humans evolved into modern humans, called *Homo sapiens*, our direct ancestors. These early people ate wild plants, and fished and hunted for food.

People in Africa learnt to spear fish with sharp sticks in lakes and rivers.

5 Arctic

Humans need particular skills to live in the freezing Arctic. Many early humans that lived here became specialists in trapping animals and hunting, or they learned to manage herds of animals, such as reindeer.

Arctic people wore heavy furs to keep warm in the cold.

People made early clay pots in Japan.

The prehistoric megafauna (giant animals) of Australia are now extinct.

6 Japan

Humans arrived in Japan about 35,000 years ago. They were the first people to make their stone axes by grinding them instead of flintknapping (shaping flint).

7 Australia

Archaeologists don't know how early people travelled to Australia, but they quickly adapted to the hot climate. They would have faced animals such as giant turtles and marsupials as big as a cow!

Ice Age

When freezing temperatures cause ice to cover large parts of the world, this is called an Ice Age. There were several Ice Ages during the Stone Age, but the last major one started about 110,000 years ago. It lasted for many thousands of years, ending around 10,000BCE. At its height, a third of the Earth was covered in ice. Living things had to learn to survive the cold. Ice Age humans made warm clothes and shelters from animal skins, fur, and bone.

The last great Ice Age started about 110,000 years ago.

About a third of the Earth was covered in ice.

Where?

Ice sheets up to 4 km (2 miles) thick could be found on five of the Earth's seven continents during the last great Ice Age. Some of this ice still exists today in Antartica and Greenland.

Danger!

In many places, temperatures stayed below freezing throughout the year. People had to find ways of protecting themselves against the cold. Food became hard to come by because few plants could grow and many animals couldn't surive.

Humans

The first humans appeared and developed in Africa about 200,000 years ago. It was during a later Ice Age, about 130,000 to 90,000 years ago, that they started to spread. Over time, they travelled across the world.

Ice Age skull of a human

The ocean waters of the Arctic in the north and Antarctic in the south were also covered in ice.

Even today, Greenland is covered in ice.

Today's ice coverage

Shelter

People in the coldest parts of the world made huts. As trees couldn't grow in freezing conditions, they used animal bones to make the frames, and draped them with animal skins.

A Ukranian animal-bone hut

Animals

Some animals from the Ice Age have been found frozen in ice after many thousands of years. As well as mammoths, people have discovered woolly rhinos, horses, bison (buffalo), cave lions, and even puppies!

Woolly bison

Clothes

Ice Age clothes were made out of animal skins, which were carefully cleaned and prepared first. Some clothes were decorated with thousands of beads. These clothes took years to make.

Ice Age shoes filled with dried grasses to help insulate from the cold.

This ancient horse breed is called Przewalski's horse and it still exists today!

Stone tools

People in the Stone Age regularly needed to cut meat, scrape skins, and cut up plants. Stone was the best and most common material around to make tools to do these tasks. The earliest tools were rocks that had been hit with great force to create sharp edges. As people began using stone tools for special tasks, different styles developed.

A straight blade was sharper than a handaxe.

Handaxes

Handaxes were one of the earliest and most popular tools in the Stone Age tool kit. They were especially useful for chopping meat, and were also used to break open bones and cut wood.

Blades

Blades were struck from larger pieces of stone. They had lots of different uses, including carving out pieces of antler and bone that could be made into other tools.

How to hold a handaxe

WOW!

People used to call **axes** **"thunderstones"** as they thought they were made by **lightning!**

Blade being used to carve an antler

Microliths

These are small, sharp points snapped off from blades. They could be attached to arrows, spears, darts, or harpoons (long spears used for fishing).

Microliths could be glued to a piece of antler to make a harpoon tip.

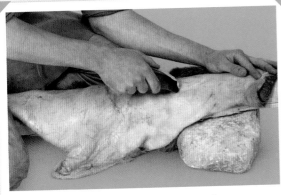

Scraper being used on an animal hide

The tip was used for scraping.

Axes

At the end of the Stone Age, people began farming. They needed more specialised axes so they could cut bigger trees to clear land. Some axes were made by carefully grinding very hard stone against rough rocks to create strong and sharp axe heads.

Scrapers

As their name suggests, scrapers were used to scrape flesh and hair from animal skins to make leather or furs. They had to be sharp enough to remove flesh, but not so sharp that they cut into the skin.

Axe being sharpened with a stone

On the hunt

Early people hunted almost anything that climbed, crawled, walked, swam, or flew. Animals were the main source of food necessary to survive in the Stone Age, especially in cold climates. This meant that people needed to invent effective weapons for hunting in order to stay alive.

Arrow points
Sharp points made of stone or bone were attached to the end of an arrow or spear to cut through animal skin.

Leaf-shaped

Fishtail-shaped

Feathered arrows

Bow string made from animal sinew (tissue)

Arrow made from hazel wood

Bows were traditionally made from wood, but some groups made them from antler and bone.

Bows held in a quiver made from rabbit skin

Bow hunting
Bows were invented near the end of the Stone Age. They needed a lot of time and effort to make, but the hunter did not have to be as close to the animal as they did with spears, so it was a safer way to hunt.

Fishing

People fished in many ways. They waded into rivers and the sea to spear fish. They also used fish traps and hooks, and worked together using nets. This hunter is using a harpoon – a spear for catching fish.

Harpoon head
The pointed end of the harpoon was called the head, and it was often decorated with plant or bird shapes.

Spear thrower
This was a stick with a hook at one end to hold a spear. By throwing the spear using the thrower, the speed, distance, and power were increased.

Spear made from hazel wood

Spear throwing

The first spears were made for thrusting. They required the hunter to get close to an animal to wound it. This could be dangerous. Then people started making spears to throw. Some groups of people made spear throwers, so spears could be thrown even further.

What did they hunt?

Big animals, such as woolly rhinoceros, were dangerous to hunt. Some groups of people specialized in catching one type of animal, such as reindeer. Smaller animals, such as frogs and turtles, were easier to catch.

In the water
Early people caught fish and other animals in rivers and in the sea. Shellfish were collected on the coast. Fish could be dried, smoked, and stored, and provided a healthy diet.

Salmon

Seal

Trees and bushes
Birds nesting in trees and bushes, such as pigeons and ptarmigans, were hunted. Squirrels were also caught.

Ptarmigan

Land
People hunted all kinds of land animals, including hares, bison, red deer, wild boar, and horses.

Red deer

Hare

Stone Age animals

Many Stone Age animals would be terrifying to humans today! Herbivores (plant-eating animals) tended to be much larger than their modern relatives, which meant that many of the carnivores (meat-eating animals) hunting them were much larger as well. Large Stone Age animals are known as megafauna.

Tooth fossil

Sabre-toothed cats

These large cats had long fangs that looked like a sabre (sword) and could be up to 50 cm (20 in) long! Their sharp teeth could even pierce the hair and hide of larger animals. The most famous species was the sabre-toothed tiger, found only in the Americas.

» Scale

Auroch skull fossil

Aurochs

The aurochs was a large ancestor of today's cows. Like modern cows, aurochs ate mostly grass. They survived much longer than most Stone Age megafauna. The last recorded example died in 1627. Aurochs are frequently seen on cave art.

» Scale

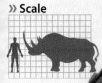

Woolly rhinoceros

Related to modern rhinos, the woolly rhinoceros had a thick coat and a compact body suited for life in the cold grasslands of Northern Europe and Asia. Some of the woolly rhino's habitat is now underwater.

A molar tooth from a woolly rhino

Cave bears

Humans had to compete with cave bears for caves to live in. These huge bears ate mainly plants. Cave bears were related to American brown bears and weighed about 450 kg (1,000 lb) or more.

» Scale

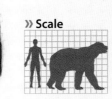

Cave bear tooth fossil

Still around today

Many of the animals that existed in the Stone Age are still with us today in a similar form to their ancestors.

Wild boar quickly adapt to new environments.

Wild horses were a big source of food in the Stone Age.

Many species of deer still exist across the world.

Mammoths

Mammoths were one of the largest land animals living during the Stone Age and are one of the best known. Related to elephants, these giant animals were adapted to cold weather and were found in North America, Europe, Africa, and Asia. Much of what we know about them comes from mammoths that have been found frozen in ice.

Thick fur coat
The fur had two layers – a long outer layer and a thick, inner layer that helped protect, or insulate, from the cold.

Baby mammoth
Mammoth babies nursed from their mothers and stayed close by until they were old enough to defend themselves.

Lyuba

Lyuba was a baby mammoth found in the Russian Arctic in 2007 by reindeer herder Yuri Khudi. The mammoth was in such good condition that they knew what her last meal was! Lyuba was named after Yuri's wife to thank him.

The 41,800-year-old Lyuba is in Shemanovsky Museum, Russia.

! WOW!

Mammoths were still alive **4,000 years ago** – when the **Egyptian pyramids** were being built!

Tiny ears
The mammoth's ears were small to prevent them being damaged from the extreme cold.

Strong, sharp tusks
Mammoths may have used their massive tusks to fight each other with and as shovels to clear snow away from the plants they ate!

Hunted animal

The mammoth was a great source of food and tools for any Stone Age hunter lucky enough to hunt one or find a dead one. Their thick hair and body fat, large bones, and tusks meant the whole animal could be used – like having a Stone Age supermarket!

Mouth
Inside the mammoth's mouth were ridges that helped grind tough plants. They acted like a conveyor belt, moving the food to the back of the mouth as they chewed!

Feet
The soles of the feet had large cracks. This gave grip in the snow, like the tread on snow boots!

Mammoth sizes

There were a number of different species of mammoth. These pictures on the right show the sizes in comparison to an adult human.

Imperial mammoth
This huge mammoth was one of the biggest species, at about 4.9 m (16 ft) tall.

Woolly mammoth
This was about the size of an African elephant, at 3.5 m (11.4 ft) tall.

Pygmy mammoth
The pygmy was one of the smallest species, at 2.1 m (6.8 ft) tall.

Making tools

Early people used stone tools to chop up meat and cut plants and animal skins. The earliest stone tools, called choppers, were simple chunks of glassy rock that were sharp on one side. People made beautifully shaped tools called handaxes. Handaxes could be used for many jobs. They were the Stone Age person's "multi-tool".

TOOLKIT

Hammer stones
These are rounded rocks used to strike the flint, causing it to split in the direction you want.

Soft hammer
Usually made of antler (deer horn), this causes the flint to break in a thinner, more regular way to make finer tools.

Shaping rocks

Flint is a hard rock found in chalk and limestone. The shaping of flint and other stones to make tools is called flintknapping. Stone Age people learnt to flintknapp from a young age. It was a skilled technique that took years to master.

The piece of rock being shaped is called the core.

Many of the flakes that come off the rock are still useful as cutting tools because they can be very sharp.

Leather clothing helped protect the flintknapper from being cut by sharp pieces of rock flying off at high speed.

1 Toolmakers had to find the right type of rock. The rock here is flint, which is ideal. People would travel far to find the right stone for their tools.

2 They began by using large hammer stones to thin and shape the rock (called the core). By hitting both sides of the rock, large pieces were removed and the shape started to emerge.

How to make a handaxe

Here's how Stone Age toolmakers shaped a handaxe from a piece of rock. They used stone, such as flint, which would break without crumbling when you struck it.

4 To thin it, the toolmaker hit the hand axe with either a smaller hard hammer, such as a pebble, or by using a soft hammer, such as a piece of deer antler.

3 The toolmakers continued to strike each side of the rock. Each strike created a flat "platform" on which to create the next strike.

Forest foods

Before farming, Stone Age people relied on the forest for food and medicines. They were highly skilled at identifying the best plants and when and how to use them. If it was edible and tasted good, Stone Age people probably ate it!

Crab apples
Stone Age people gathered wild apples, such as crab apples. People of central Asia were they first to grow apples as crops.

Hawthorn
The berries stay on the trees late into winter and the tender leaves are eaten in the spring.

Plums
Full of natural sugar, many varieties of wild plum were gathered by Stone Age people.

Fruit
Wild fruit was the easiest source of sugar for early people. Children especially may well have enjoyed eating the sweet, ripe fruit. When people brought fruit back to camp, they would have scattered fruit seeds unintentionally, and so encouraged fruit to grow near their camps.

Sloe berries
These berries become very sweet after a frost. Otzi the Iceman had them in his stomach.

Blackberries
Blackberries grew wild and their brambles made good cordage (rope).

Elderflower
The berries need cooking before eating, and were usually made into drinks.

Poisonous plants

Stone Age people learned from experience to avoid poisonous plants. Some plants are not just poisonous to eat but may even be poisonous to touch. Remember to stay away from poisonous plants!

Holly berries
Colourful holly berries may be beautiful, but eating only a few will make both people and animals very sick.

Burdock
This plant has tasty and nutritious roots that are still eaten or brewed in tea.

Dandelions
Highly nutritious, dandelions are often cooked like spinach.

Rosehips
High in vitamin C, this fruit can be dried and later used in winter.

Sorrel
Slightly sour, sorrel leaves are eaten worldwide.

Plants

Stone Age humans did not just eat meat. Plants made up a large part of many people's diets. Early people may also have used plants as medicine. The willow bark, for instance, contains the same painkilling ingredient found in aspirin.

Acorns
Most acorns have bitter chemicals called tannins that have to be removed by grinding and boiling them.

Walnuts
Walnuts are very nutritious and full of good fats.

Nettle
Nettle leaves lose their sting when cooked and are good in soups or toasted.

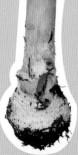

Yew
Yew wood has been used to make tools for at least 400,000 years, but almost all parts of it are poisonous to humans and animals.

Fly agaric
This classic toadstool contains a poison that can kill in high doses. Early people would have known to stay well away.

Deadly nightshade
Despite having an attractive berry, this plant has been used to make poison for thousands of years.

Shelter

Stone Age people needed good shelters to protect themselves from bad weather. Animal-skin huts were among the earliest types of shelter built. The frames were made from thin, flexible tree branches, and animal skins were draped over them. The materials were light enough to carry easily, making them ideal for the typical hunter-gatherer, who was always on the move.

Flexible wooden poles often made from ash or hazel for the frame

Simple containers to carry food and tools

Deer-skin hut

This hut is a recreation of a Stone Age shelter, and was made from about 40 roe-deer skins. Animal skin was ideal material for hut walls, as it trapped in the heat, so the insides were dry and warm. It was also easy to repair.

The top layers of skins overlapped the lower layers to keep water out.

Deer skin covered the floor for warmth.

Axe for cutting poles

Extra clothing and animal-skin blankets

What's inside

Take a peek inside this deer-skin tent to find out what you'd see in a typical Stone Age shelter. Woven baskets were handy for storage. Animal-skin blankets covered the floor, helping to keep the tent snug and warm.

! WOW!

Stone Age **roof-thatching techniques** are still used for houses in some parts of the world **today!**

Other shelters

While many people used animal skins to build their shelter, others used dried grasses. Caves were popular because they didn't have to be built!

Cave in Mongolia

Cave life

Caves offered immediate protection from wind, rain, and snow. But many were dark and damp and there was always the danger that animals, such as bears, lived there.

Humans and cave bears may have competed for the same cave.

Shelter made from grasses, England

Grass shelter

Simple grass shelters were used by some Stone Age groups during the winter. The careful layering of grasses is called thatching, and helps hold in heat.

Fire

Fire-making is a very ancient skill and one of the most important of the Stone Age. Once people started using fire, it provided many advantages. Fire helped people to keep warm, cook food, and to provide light for work in the evening.

Warmth

A warm fire is cozy and comforting to sit around, but for early humans this warmth would have been crucial for survival, especially in cold climates.

How people made fire

Early humans came across wild fires in forests, and then gradually learned how to make it themselves. One method of making fire using various handmade tools is called the bow drill.

The drill is a thick, pencil-shaped stick.

Step 1
A small nest from dried grass, called tinder, was made. Small pieces of dry wood, called kindling, were collected. These would be used to catch the first flame.

Piece of wood, called a hearth, with notches cut into it

Piece of wood to protect the hand

Bow made from flexible hazel wood

Nest of dried grass, called tinder

Small, dry sticks of wood, called kindling

Light

Fire gave early people light, which is important because our eyes do not see well in the dark. Having light allowed people to hunt and find shelters at night. It let people explore deep caves that gave good shelter.

Protection

Fire helped protect early humans from predatory animals, such as wolves or bears. They would have been scared of the light from the fire.

Grey wolf

Cooking

Eating cooked food helped to make people healthier, as food that has been cooked carries less disease. Cooked food is also quicker and easier to digest. The extra energy may have helped the brain to grow bigger, too.

Cooking pot

Step 2
The tip of the drill was placed into one of the notches of the hearth. The bow string was wrapped around the drill. The drill was spun by moving the bow back and forth.

Step 3
As the fire-maker spun the drill faster, smoke appeared, and a red-hot ember formed. He then placed the burning ember by hand into the tinder bundle and blew on it.

Step 4
He continued to blow on the ember until it burst into a small flame. He set it on the ground and added the kindling, until it flared into a crackling fire.

Piece of wood to protect the hand

Bow looped around drill

Ember starts to smoke

Place the burning ember on the ground

A day in the life

During the Stone Age, it is believed that people lived together in close-knit groups of about three or four families. Children helped out with everyday jobs from an early age. This story imagines what life would have been like for a young girl called Tiya ...

The families had arrived at their summer camp. Tiya helped her grandmother put up the frame of their shelter. They used long flexible branches from the hazel tree and draped them with animal skins.

That night, the hunters returned with their prize – a young bison. This would feed the group for weeks!

Some of the group were preparing to go hunting. Tiya wanted to join in, but she was too young just yet. She took a spear and started practising.

There were great celebrations around the campfire that night. The group sang songs and told stories. They played flutes made from bone and mammoth ivory.

Suddenly, Tiya heard rustling in the trees. She crept away to investigate and spied a wolverine! Though small, it was known to kill prey larger than itself.

Tiya knew she had to think quickly. She grabbed a spear, and hurled it. The animal stumbled and fell.

Tiya's grandmother led the group in congratulating Tiya for being brave and quick-thinking. She was now ready to join the next hunt.

Taming wolves

About 30,000 years ago, early people started to live and work alongside Stone Age wolves. These early wolves looked and behaved in similar ways to today's wolves. Over thousands of years, early wolves developed into the many breeds of dogs that we see today.

Wolves today

Stone Age wolves probably looked very similar to today's grey wolves, but they were even larger.

How it happened

Wolves were naturally drawn to early human settlements. They became used to searching for waste that people had left out, or even began to steal food.

Round the campfire
Some groups got used to having wolves nearby. They scared away predatory animals. Some wolves may have followed human camps.

Wolves and cubs
As wolves got used to being near people, they started to have their cubs nearby. Some people began feeding the friendlier cubs and wolves.

FACT FILE

» **Name:** grey wolf, also called the timber wolf

» **Habitat:** colder climates in the northern hemisphere (half) of the world

» **Diet:** large and small animals; occasionally fruits and berries

Wolf cubs tamed

Gradually, wolf cubs were adopted and tamed by people. These adopted wolves bred with each other, gradually creating a new species.

Living together

Stone Age people used these early tamed wolves to hunt with. The dogs also acted as guards and companions.

Stone Age clothes

Just as we do today, early people needed clothes to keep warm. In later Stone Age times, clothes were made from grasses and plant stems that were woven together to make fabric. Animal hides were also worn, and were especially useful in cold weather.

Leather outfit

This woman is wearing a tunic and trousers made from softened deer skin. Leather is very hardwearing, while giving protection from cold winds.

Necklace made from animal bones

Container made from tree bark

Legs stayed warm in leather trousers

There were no concrete pavements in Stone Age times, and people could quite easily walk on earth and grass in bare feet.

Summer worker

This woman is wearing a tunic made from the flax plant. At the end of the Stone Age, clothes woven from flax fibre were found to be ideal for keeping cool in warmer weather and for working.

Long sticks, called digging sticks, were used to dig up vegetables and roots. The stick was burnt at either end to make the points harder, so both ends could be used.

This spearhead is made from a rock called flint. Other spearheads were made from bone, antler, or ivory.

! WOW!

Some clothes were woven from the stems of **stinging nettles!**

Winter hunter

In the cold winter months, Stone Age people wore animal skins, such as this tunic made from red deer skin. Skins kept them warm while out hunting.

The dull brown colour of the fur made great camouflage in woodland.

The belt has a pouch at the front for carrying stone tools.

This backpack is made from deer skin. The wooden frame is similar to metal frames found in modern rucksacks.

Spears were made from hazel or ash wood.

Shoes made from deer skin were sometimes worn to keep warm in the cold winter.

Needle and thread

Towards the end of the Stone Age, the needle and thread were invented to help make clothes. Once people could wear fitted clothing, it was easier for them to keep warm and to live in harsher climates.

Needles were made from bone and threaded with plant fibre.

How to survive the Stone Age

Klint Janulis, a former American Special Forces soldier, is now a survival instructor and Stone Age archaeologist at the University of Oxford, England. Klint studies how people survived in the Stone Age and how modern hunter-gatherer groups live to look for clues about how humans lived in the past.

FACT FILE

» **Name:** Klint Janulis

» **Born:** 17 March 1980

» **Favourite Stone Age tool:** Acheulean hand axe – "The Stone Age multi-tool"

» **Special skills:** survival, hunting, flintknapping, building shelters

Make a good shelter

"Surviving the Stone Age required technical skills, social skills, and intelligence. Knowing how to make a good shelter was essential. This could be made from leaves and grasses, animal skins, or if you were lucky, you might find a cosy cave."

Klint made this shelter from dried grass.

Hunting and trapping

"Stone Age people understood their environment – what plants they could eat, what types of wood were best for spears, where deer liked to bed down at night. Hunting and trapping animals, and fishing, were vital skills. For a Stone Age child, play was made up of learning the skills to hunt and trap."

Klint weaving a fish-catching basket

Fish-catching basket

Make fire

"Making fire was one of the most important Stone Age skills. It kept you warm, scared away dangerous animals, and cooked your food. Using fire in the Stone Age was as important as knowing how to use a computer today."

Make friends

"We make friends by helping each other out and sharing. Making friends in the Stone Age gave you advantages. If you wanted to hunt a large herd of animals, your friends and neighbours could help out."

Think ahead

"Early people learnt how to plan for the future. This included storing extra food for later, when food was scarce. This is similar to people today saving money in the bank instead of spending it straightaway."

Grain could be stored

Beliefs

We can find out a lot about early people's beliefs by the burial sites they left behind. The dead were buried with tools and jewellery that would have taken months to make. Great ruins such as Stonehenge tell us that people were thinking about more than just hunting and gathering food.

Megalith

A megalith is a huge stone, or a collection of stones, that were used to mark a sacred place. The word comes from two Greek words meaning "big" and "rock".

Shamans may have worn animal skins to show their status.

Shamanism

Shamans were people who looked after the spiritual and physical wellbeing of the group. They held rituals to keep the community safe from evil spirits and used medicinal plants to treat illness.

Animal carving from Göbekli Tepe, Anatolia, Turkey

Göbekli Tepe

Göbekli Tepe is one of the most important Stone Age finds. It is a large series of stone buildings that have carvings of animals on them. It may have been a religious temple.

Most megaliths consist of several huge stones fitted together without cement.

Stonehenge

This circle of standing stones called Stonehenge is surrounded in mystery. Nobody knows exactly why Stonehenge was built or how it was used. It may have been a sacred monument, a burial site, a centre for healing, or acted as a calendar.

Stonehenge, Wiltshire, England

Newgrange burial mound, County Meath, Ireland

Burial mound

At the end of the Stone Age, people were sometimes buried in burial mounds. These were large mounds of earth containing graves. They have been found all over the world.

Burial objects

The earliest objects to be buried with the dead were stone tools and red ochre (a mineral used to make paint). Jewellery and traces of wild flowers have also been found.

Bone necklace

Amazing find

The Lascaux cave paintings are about 17,000 years old. They were discovered by accident in 1940, when four teenage boys followed their dog into a hole in the ground. They rescued the dog and found the cave! The paintings show cattle, horses, and other animals painted in reds, yellows, and browns.

Cow painted in red ochre

Horse painted in brown ochre

Cave painting

Thousands of years ago, the first artists painted colourful scenes inside caves. Among the most famous paintings are those found in Lascaux in southwest France. Many of the paintings show animals that people hunted for food. Stone Age artists looked closely at the animals and drew them very carefully and accurately.

WOW!

Early people **blew paint** through **hollow bird wing bones,** making the first **spray paint!**

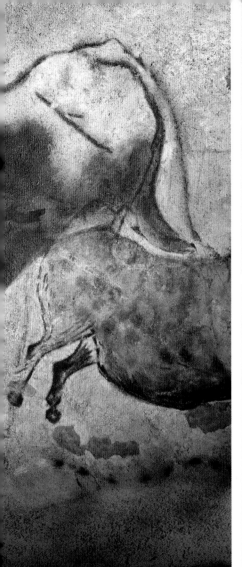

Human figures rarely appear in cave paintings, but here you can see an outline of a person with a bird-like head.

Deer can be seen in many of the Lascaux paintings. The one here is called "the running deer". Its long antlers can be clearly seen.

Natural colours

Early artists made their paints from natural materials, such as ochre, a mineral found in the earth. Ochre was ground into a powder, then mixed with water or animal fats to create paint.

Yellow ochre pebble

Charcoal (burnt wood) was used for black.

Crushed red ochre in a shell

Painting tools

Early people painted using brushes, much like artists today. To spread paint over large areas, they used leather pads filled with moss or grass.

Leather pad filled with moss

Horsehair brush gave a heavier coat of paint.

Goose feather paintbrush was used for lighter coats.

Caves of the world

Stone Age humans often made their homes in caves because they provided a ready made house and were often close to water, which would attract animals. People decorated these caves with magnificent prehistoric paintings, many showing animals. The artists may have painted to celebrate success at hunting or as a way of communicating with the spirit world.

Red buffalo
These cave paintings in Altamira Cave were the first ever found. They show animals including horses, goats, and buffalo. The paintings changed the way early people were viewed. Up until then, people did not think that early people could draw and paint.

Altamira Cave, Cantabria, Spain

Cave of Hands (Cueva de las Manos), Santa Cruz, Argentina

Cave of Hands
Early people in Argentina created these wonderful outlines of hands. They placed their hands on the wall and blew paint over the wall to create the painting. It may have been a way of leaving a signature or sign, perhaps for the spirit world.

Bhimbetka rock shelters, Madhya Pradesh, India

Hunters on horseback
Early people in India painted this scene showing men on horseback hunting with spears. These paintings are the earliest ever found in India.

The rock shelters shown from the outside

Warriors and dancers
Stone Age artists painted over a million pictures on rocks in the Kimberley region of Australia. Many show human figures hunting, running, or dancing, carrying bags, and wearing tassels and headdresses. These paintings are over 20,000 years old.

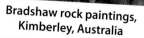
Bradshaw rock paintings, Kimberley, Australia

Stone Age detective

Archaeologists do more than dig up artefacts. To find out about life in the past, they use some of the same techniques as police detectives. For example, using chemicals to date artefacts tells us how old a material is or when it last saw sunlight. Archaeologists also make replicas (models) of Stone Age tools to find out how our ancestors might have used them.

The very dry landscape and geology in the Olduvai Gorge helped to preserve the Stone Age tools and fossils.

Olduvai Gorge

In the Olduvai Gorge in Tanzania, Africa, archaeologists have found traces of early humans that are more than 2 million years old. These include some of the earliest evidence of humans using tools to chop up animals, discovered from cut marks on animal bones.

Neolithic bowl

At the end of the Stone Age, pottery became more common to hold crops and food. By analysing remains left in the pottery, such as dried food, archaeologists can work out what people ate. Similar pottery styles also help us to link cultures and communities.

Spiral meander design

Making stone tools required intelligence and skill. By studying how tools were made, archaeologists can determine the abilities of our early ancestors.

"The hobbit"

Often called "the hobbit" due to its small size, remains of this human relative were found on an island off the coast of Indonesia, where the water is very deep. Archaeologists are trying to work out how these people got to the island and why they were so small.

"The hobbit" skull

Markers show rock layers for studying (stratigraphy)

Digging deep

A basic rule of archaeology is that older stuff sits under newer stuff. Think of a messy bedroom with clothes piled on top of toys. The toys on the bottom of the pile have probably been there longer than the clothes on top! In this picture, the shells at the bottom have been there longer than the shells at the top.

Cheddar Man

Cheddar Man is the name given to a body found in a cave in Cheddar Gorge, England, a place famous for its cheese. The caves in the gorge have a constant temperature, making them ideal for ageing cheese as well as providing a comfortable home for Stone Age humans.

Cheddar Man's skeleton

REALLY?

DNA evidence shows that **Cheddar Man** is a distant ancestor of some people living there today.

Meet the expert

Dr Beccy Scott works at the British Museum in London, England. She is particularly interested in Neanderthals and is trying to find out how they survived in the area around the English Channel by studying their stone tools in detail.

Q: Could you explain what an archaeologist does?

A: Archaeologists use the traces (pieces) people leave behind to recreate what their lives were like. We might excavate (dig) the sites where they lived and recover objects that they left behind: stone tools, pottery, animal bones. We then study these things in detail – to see how they were made, and what they were used for.

Q: What inspired you to become an archaeologist?

A: I grew up near the chalk hills of Kent, England, so I was always collecting flints, trying to make arrowheads, and trying to find monuments marked on maps.

Q: What do you enjoy most about being an archaeologist?

A: I enjoy fieldwork the best. When you're digging, it brings you close to the people we're studying. You're recreating the actions of someone thousands of years ago. It can feel a bit spooky!

Q: What do you love about studying the Stone Age in particular?

A: I love that we only have evidence that Stone Age people left us to understand how they lived. It means you need a good imagination to open your mind to all possibilities!

Chalk cliffs on the coast of Kent, England, where Beccy grew up

Beccy enjoyed trying to make arrowheads as a child.

Q: What things have you learnt about Stone Age people?

A: I mostly study the Neanderthals, and they never cease to surprise me. Archaeologists used to write about them as if they were hardly human. We now know that they were people just like us – they just had different ways of living.

Q: What is your most amazing find?

A: The find I'm proudest of is a henge! It was hard to see at first because the ditch was infilled with gravel. I was really pleased – not just that we'd found it, but that I'd stuck to my guns when no one believed me!

Q: Could you describe a typical day in your work?

A: If I'm in the field, then we get up early and spend the day on site digging. We remove sediment carefully with trowels, leaving all the stone tools exactly where we found them. Then we plot exactly where the tools are, and lift them one at a time. They go straight into bags with all the details of where they came from written on them. When we get back to our camp in the evening we make sure these details are put onto computers.

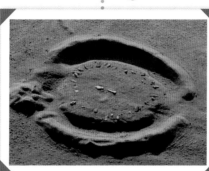

A henge is a Neolithic monument with a circular ditch and bank. This henge is in Derbyshire, England.

Q: What sort of equipment do you use?

A: It depends what I'm doing. We use shovels and mattocks, or pickaxes, then trowels, and finally, if you're cleaning around delicate bones or flints, we might use plastic tools. We hardly ever use brushes, despite what you see in films!

Q: What is the most difficult part of your job?

A: I'm not a very patient person, and sometimes you have to be patient as an archaeologist. It takes time to excavate carefully. You need to finish what you're doing, understand it, and then move on.

Q: Do you have any advice for future archaeologists?

A: Look at everything like an archaeologist! When you go to the beach, see how people choose to sit around, and the marks that they leave behind. How do the marks relate to what you saw? Imagine finding the contents of your pockets in the future: what would rot away, and what would people think about you based on what survived? You don't have to dig holes to be an archaeologist – it's a way of looking at people through things.

Plastic tool

Trowel

Mattock

Ends used for digging and chopping

Crop farming

Among the first crops to be farmed were peas, lentils, and wheat. These could all be stored for a long time. Having extra food that was stored gave people a much better chance of surviving a hard winter or a drought.

Grinding stone

Shifting to farming meant that new stone tools were needed. People began using coarse stones to grind grains into flour.

Planting seeds at the right time of year was very important.

Instead of planning around the yearly hunt, a farmer's life now focused on the harvest.

Farmers learned to dig canals to route water from lakes and rivers towards their fields. Some early canals are still in use today!

Farmers chopped down trees and used the wood for tools and to make fires.

First farmers

Towards the end of the Stone Age, people started to farm in many parts of the world. Some settled down in fixed houses to plant crops and raise farm animals. Others kept small farms but continued to hunt and gather for most of their food. As farming developed and changed, so did the plants and animals that were being farmed.

Animal farming

Farming animals had advantages over hunting them. It provided a source of goods from the same animal all year round. To keep an animal such as a goat meant that you constantly had milk, and could cut its wool each year for clothing.

Some groups raised animals but were still nomadic, travelling from place to place.

Shepherds needed to keep a careful watch of their sheep to keep them safe.

Wild pigs were domesticated and kept in pens.

People used the flat roofs of houses as extra living space.

People cooked meat from the animals they raised on open fires.

Goats could be raised in dryer climates, as they needed little water.

REALLY?

! All **large farm animals** share an important trait – they all **live in herds that have leaders.**

Stone Age village

A village in the Stone Age was quite different to a village today. People relied on each other for getting food and putting up shelters, and worked together as a group throughout the year. Not only did villagers know each other very well, but they lived closely together and would probably have been related.

Skara Brae

Skara Brae is a Neolithic (New Stone Age) site in the Orkney Islands. It was made almost entirely out of local rocks that are wide, flat, and stack very easily, making them ideal for building. The buildings give an amazing glimpse of Neolithic life!

WHAT'S INSIDE

1 **Fire hearth** The fire was in the centre of the house, allowing everyone to gather around. Dried seaweed or peat may have been burnt.

2 **Flat stones** This site had very few trees to build with, but there were plenty of flat stones to build anything from walls to furniture.

3 **Outside** The houses were built into piles of waste with grass on top. This provided insulation against the cold climate.

4 **Stone dressers** Located in the same position in each house, these may have been used to show off goods or for religious purposes.

5 **Stone boxes** These were waterproofed with clay. People may have stored live limpets in the boxes to use as fishing bait.

6 **Stone beds** Animal hides and coverings would have made the beds more comfortable. Each house had one large bed and one small bed.

The Orkney Islands are located off the coast of Scotland in the British Isles.

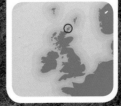

Village life

Many early Stone Age villages had shelters that could be moved easily so that people could follow animal herds for food and skins. Villagers may have come from different related families who lived apart some of the time and then came together for the hunting season. People would have needed to meet people from other villages and groups to find partners for mating!

A typical Stone Age village

4

5

3

1

6

WOW!

For more than **5,000 years, Skara Brae** was buried in the earth. In 1850, a **powerful storm** revealed the **Stone Age village.**

Arts and crafts

Weaving, sculpting, or basket-making are among the many arts and crafts that people enjoy today. But for early people, they were necessary tools for survival. The ability to make things gave people an advantage over those who could not. For instance, making a basket meant you could carry a lot more berries home.

This bone necklace was strung together with leather or flax; holes were made with a simple drill made of flint.

Bone and antler

Bone and antler provided ideal material for early humans to carve with. It was easy to work, harder-wearing than wood, and there was lots of it. Things made from bone and antler included needles, jewellery, and even shelters!

This stone ball is carved from volcanic rock and took about a year to make.

Stone carving of a mammoth

Stone

This was one of the first materials to be crafted by humans. The first things to be made were tools for cutting. By the end of the Stone Age, people were making a wide variety of objects, such as arrowheads, containers, figurines, and jewellery.

This late Stone Age marble figure is from Greece.

These stone earrings come from China.

This clay animal may have been a child's toy.

Clay

Once Stone Age people started to settle they began to use clay to make containers. Clay pots were useful to cook food in and to hold dried food to protect it from animal scavengers. Groups that moved around a lot did not often keep pottery.

Heavy clay pots were used by settled communities.

Tree bark

People used bark from trees, such as birch and cedar, to make lightweight containers. These allowed people to carry food or water long distances and to store it for future use. Thicker wood from oak trees was useful for making axe handles.

Containers were made from bark or from woven grasses.

How people made rope

Rope-making (cordage) was one of the most important Stone Age crafts. It helped people to make containers, traps, and snares for catching animals. People could sew clothes, stitch together skins for shelters, and tie bundles together.

1 **Find the right plant**
The right plant needed to be found: one with long, thin, strong fibres, such as the nettle plant, shown here, was ideal.

2 **Prepare the stems**
The leaves were stripped from the stems of the nettle plant. While taking care not to get stung, each stem was then crushed with the thumb to soften it.

3 **Strip the stems**
The outer parts from the stems were carefully removed. The inner stem fibres were then left to dry out thoroughly.

4 **Twist the stems**
The fibres were twisted or plaited so that they tightened against each other and became strong.

Bronze Age

The Bronze Age describes a period in time when some societies learned to produce tools made from bronze. At the same time, these societies become more dependent on farming and trade. The Bronze Age did not occur at the same time for all societies, but generally the Bronze Age followed the late Stone Age.

! WOW!

Thank the Bronze Age that you're **reading** this! It was at this time that **writing** and **counting systems** were **developed!**

What is bronze?

Bronze is a mixture of two metals: copper and tin. When mixed together these two metals are both harder and more long-lasting than they are by themselves.

Hot, melting bronze being poured

Why was it so special?

Bronze is made from materials that were easy to mine. It is also an easy metal to melt and mould into shape. Bronze tools, such as axes and swords, were harder and more hard-wearing than stone tools.

Mould for bronze pins

Finished pin in bronze

Weapons

Bronze Age societies were often at war with each other and this made bronze swords and armour important for their effectiveness when fighting.

Tools

Bronze tools, such as axes, were necessary to help clear land for farming. Flint tools were still being used by some Bronze Age people, but not to the extent they were in the Stone Age.

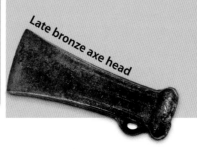

Late bronze axe head

Flint knife

Jewellery

Bronze Age jewellery was worn by the fashionable. Increases in farming and trade meant that some people became very wealthy. They used that wealth the same way some people do today, by owning jewellery.

Bronze bracelet

Bronze ring

Sussex loops were bracelets that were bent double to form a loop.

When left out in the air, bronze oxidizes and turns green.

Bronze handle

Bronze sword

Trade

Farming and bronze tool-making became big business in the Bronze Age. This encouraged the trading of new foods, clothes, and jewellery among societies across the world. It also created the need for an early form of coins – slabs of copper, or ingots, which had a standard value.

Copper ingot

Travel

Bronze Age societies began travelling further to buy and sell their goods. They built advanced ships and learnt how to find their way (navigate) across great distances.

Rock carving from Sweden showing a boat

Roundhouse

A roundhouse is a house that is circular, usually with a cone-shaped roof. This style of house was found throughout Europe during the Iron Age. There was just one room inside, with a fire in the centre, used for cooking and eating.

Thatched roof
Thatch made from straw provided a long-lasting way to protect, or insulate, a house and keep the snow and rain out.

Doorway
The large doorway let light in and was made big enough for animals to enter.

Iron Age

During the Iron Age, people started using tools and weapons made of iron instead of bronze. Iron is the most common metal on Earth. Iron tools have a sharper edge and are more durable than bronze. To make iron tools, raw iron from the Earth was heated in furnaces in a process called smelting. The advance in tools and weapons also led to changes in the way people lived.

! WOW!

Some of the first **iron tools** were made from **meteorites**, which means they came from **outer space**!

Hill fort

A hill fort was an Iron Age village built on a hill, surrounded by walls made of earth and stone. The view from the hilltop meant that people could spot enemies approaching and defend the fort from attack. Many hill forts were also used to house animals.

Maiden Castle
This is a hill fort in Dorset, England, which was built during the middle of the Iron Age. About the size of 50 football pitches, it was one of the largest hill forts in Europe.

Walls
The walls were usually made of stone or mud, to insulate against the cold. However, inside would have been dark and smoky.

Farming tools
Iron farm tools allowed farmers to clear the land much more efficiently than bronze. This meant farmers could produce more food with the same amount of work.

A plough pulled by a team of oxen was the Iron Age equivalent of a tractor.

Weapons
Iron weapons were stronger and sharper than bronze ones, but required more care because they could rust.

Iron Age dagger in sheath

Model of plough

Today's hunter-gatherers

A hunter-gatherer is someone who gets their food from searching, or foraging, for wild plants and hunting wild animals. We all have ancestors that were hunter-gatherers. Today, there are just a few hunter-gatherer societies left. These people are highly skilled and take time to relax as well as work.

FACT FILE

» **Name:** Hadza tribe

» **Location:** East Africa

» **Food:** plant roots, berries, baobob fruit, meat, honey, eggs

» **Language:** Khoison (a language that uses click sounds)

» **Country:** Tanzania, Serengeti, and Rift Valley

Hadza tribe

The Hadza people of East Africa are one of the last hunter-gatherer groups in the world. There are less than 1,000 Hadza people left and even fewer who still live as hunter-gatherers. These people have no written language, but have a fantastic history passed on by storytelling.

Hadza shelter
The Hadza move camps often, to adjust to the changing seasons and depending on what food is available. They can build a new shelter in an afternoon.

Poisonous arrow
This Hadza hunter is using a knife to shape and sharpen an arrow. He will then add plant poisons to the arrow tip.

Honey gatherers
The Hadza people have a special relationship with a bird called a "honey guide" bird. The bird leads the hunter to a beehive. On collecting the honey, they share this with the bird.

Camp fire
The Hadza pass the history of their people on by telling stories round the camp fire. These stories stretch back thousands of years.

Stone Age facts and figures

What we know about the Stone Age comes from the finds that archaeologists have dug up. Impress your friends with these amazing facts!

Ibex

Neanderthals had **large noses** to help them breathe in the cold air.

Obsidian is SHARPEST material on Earth!

Stone Age people used obsidian to produce very sharp blades. Today, it is still used for delicate surgery!

THE LAST MEAL

Otzi was a 5,000 year old man discovered in the Austrian Alps. His last meal was ibex (wild goat). Remains of it were found in his stomach, along with venison, grain, and berries.

3 A mammoth tusk could grow up to about 3 m (10 ft) in length.

Part of a fossilised mammoth tusk

Adult hand

11

There have been 11 Ice Ages over the last 4.6 billion years.

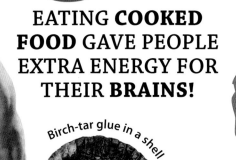

EATING COOKED FOOD GAVE PEOPLE EXTRA ENERGY FOR THEIR **BRAINS!**

A Neanderthal's brain was bigger than a modern human's!

Birch-tar glue in a shell

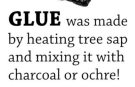

GLUE was made by heating tree sap and mixing it with charcoal or ochre!

Homo sapiens means "**wise man**"

MEGALITH

MEANS "**BIG ROCK**"

100

The longest Ice Age lasted more than 100 million years!

40,800

The oldest cave painting is El Castillo in northern Spain. It is 40,800 years old!

Glossary

Here are the meanings of some words that are useful for you to know when learning about the Stone Age.

antler Special kind of bone growth on the heads of male deer that can be used to make tools, such as soft hammers or needles

beliefs Set of views that people hold about the world, life, and the afterlife

blade Type of stone tool that is long and has a very sharp edge

cordage Similar to rope, and usually made from plant or animal fibres, it can be used to make containers, shelters, and clothing

digging stick Long stick used to dig up roots and vegetables that grow under the soil

drill Narrow piece of wood spun on a hearth board (*see* hearth) to create enough heat to make fire

evolution Gradual process by which living things change over time to adapt to their environment

A flintknapper at work

foraging Gathering food that grows wild in nature

flax Plant that has natural fibres in it that can be made into cloth or cordage

flint Type of sedimentary rock that is very glassy, and produces a sharp edge when knapped

flintknapping *See* knapping

hammer stone Hard, rounded rock used to make stone tools, such as handaxes, out of glassy rocks like flint

handaxe Stone tools that could be used for cutting and chopping

harpoon Type of spear that is used when hunting from a boat on the water

hearth The place a fire burns in a shelter and the board used with a drill to make fire

horn Made out of the same stuff as your fingernails, horns grow on the heads of some grass-eating animals.

human Also called *Homo sapiens*, humans originated in Africa and have been around for at least 200,000 years

hunter-gatherer People who get their food by gathering plants or hunting animals rather than through settled farming

Ice Age Period of time when the world is much colder, and many parts are covered in glaciers

kindling Dry, thin sticks of wood that can take the fire from the tinder and turn it into a bigger flame

knapping Process of creating stone tools by striking stone to remove material

megafauna Large animals such as elephants, woolly mammoth, and giant sloths. Many Stone Age megafauna are extinct today

megalithic Any structure made by using very large stones, such as Stonehenge or Göbekli Tepe

meteorite Pieces of rock from space that land on Earth. Some meteorites are made of solid metal and Stone Age people used them to make tools

microlith Small stone tools used to make the points of spears and arrows

Microliths attached to a harpoon tip

Neanderthal These were our closest relatives and they died out 24,000 years ago

Neolithic Time period after the Mesolithic period when humans began growing crops and raising animals

obsidian Type of volcanic rock that is extremely glassy and very sharp, and was used to make cutting tools and ornaments

ochre Mineral that has a vivid colour, which is used for paint and dye when mixed with fat

Palaeolithic Longest time period of the Stone Age, when humans learned how to make stone tools, fire, and hunt

scraper Simple stone tool used for scraping animal skins or wood to smooth them down

shaman Priest or spiritual leader who is believed to have special powers and uses them to guide people on important matters

soft hammer Softer than a hard hammer, and often made of antler or wood, the soft hammer allows a knapper to make a more precise and thin stone tool

spear thrower Tool for throwing a spear or dart a great distance with accuracy. The thrower acts as an extension of the arm giving more power

thatching Technique for making a waterproof roof out of grasses and reeds

tinder Thin material that catches fire easily

tusk Long tooth that grows from the jaws of animals such as warthogs, elephants, and mammoths. Sometimes called ivory, it can be carved easily and used to make jewellery and sculptures

wolverine Ferocious animal that is in the weasel family and mainly scavenges meat. Wolverines appear frequently in Stone Age art

Index

Acknowledgements

The publisher would like to thank the following people for their assistance in the preparation of this book: Dr Beccy Scott of The British Museum for the "Meet the expert" interview; Gary Ombler for photography; Andy Maxted of Royal Pavilion & Museums; Arran Lewis, Molly Lattin, and Dan Crisp for illustration, James Dilley (model & consultant) AncientCraft, Centre for the Archaeology of Human Origins, University of Southampton; Josie Mills and Tabitha Paterson for modelling; Cory Cuthbertson, Palaeolithic Researcher, Centre for the Archaeology of Human Origins, University of Southampton; Sally-Ann Spence of Oxford University Museum of Natural History; Neeraj Bhatia, Senior DTP Designer, and Nand Kishor Acharya, DTP Designer, for cut-out images; Garima Sharma and Surya Deogun for additional design.

The publisher would like to thank the following for their kind permission to reproduce their photographs:

(Key: a-above; b-below/bottom; c-centre; f-far; l-left; r-right; t-top)

1 Dorling Kindersley: James Dilley / www.ancientcraft.co.uk. **2 Dorling Kindersley:** Royal Pavilion & Museums, Brighton & Hove (bc). **3 Dorling Kindersley:** James Dilley / www.ancientcraft.co.uk (bl, bc, br); Royal Pavilion & Museums, Brighton & Hove (tr, cb). **4 Dorling Kindersley:** James Dilley / www.ancientcraft.co.uk (cr, fcr); Royal Pavilion & Museums, Brighton & Hove (crb). **5 Dorling Kindersley:** James Dilley / www.ancientcraft.co.uk (cla); Royal Pavilion & Museums, Brighton & Hove (tl, cra, clb, crb). **6 Dorling Kindersley:** James Dilley / www.ancientcraft.co.uk (tc, ca, c, r); Royal Pavilion & Museums, Brighton & Hove (cb). **7 123RF.com:** cobalt (bc); windu (cl). **Dorling Kindersley:** Royal Pavilion & Museums, Brighton & Hove (cr); Greg Ward / Rough Guides (tc). **8-9 Dorling Kindersley:** Dan Crisp. **10 Dorling Kindersley:** Natural History Museum, London (br). **11 123RF.com:** amadeus542 (crb/ice cube, fbr/ice cube). **Alamy Stock Photo:** Dennis Cox (fbr/horse). **Dorling Kindersley:** James Dilley / www.ancientcraft.co.uk (bc). **Getty Images:** CM Dixon / Print Collector (cra). **12 Dorling Kindersley:** James Dilley / www.ancientcraft.co.uk (tr, bl); Royal Pavilion & Museums, Brighton & Hove (cr, c, bc). **13 Dorling Kindersley:** James Dilley / www.ancientcraft.co.uk (tl, tc, tr). **14 Dorling Kindersley:** James Dilley / www.ancientcraft.co.uk (tr). **15 123RF.com:** Raldi Somers / gentoomultimedia (fcrb). **Dorling Kindersley:** British Wildlife Centre, Surrey, UK (fbr); James Dilley / www.ancientcraft.co.uk (tl, cl, bl); Royal Pavilion & Museums, Brighton & Hove (c). **16 Dorling Kindersley:** Natural History Museum, London (cra); Chester Ong (cl/background, b/background); Winsor & Newton (ftr); Royal Pavilion & Museums, Brighton & Hove (clb). **17 Dorling Kindersley:** British Wildlife Centre, Surrey, UK (br); Chester Ong (t/background, bl/background); Natural History Museum, London (fcra); Royal Pavilion & Museums, Brighton & Hove (bl); ZSL Whipsnade Zoo (cr); Chris Christoforou / Rough Guides (fcrb). **18 Alamy Stock Photo:** Vitaly Nevar / ITAR-TASS Photo Agency / Alamy Live News (bl). **20 Dorling Kindersley:** James Dilley / www.ancientcraft.co.uk (c, tr, ftr, cra). **21 Dorling Kindersley:** James Dilley / www.ancientcraft.co.uk (tl, tr, bl, br). **23 Alamy Stock Photo:** Flowerphotos (tl); Alfio Scisetti (cr). **24 Dorling Kindersley:** James Dilley / www.ancientcraft.co.uk (b); Jerry Young (cr). **24-25 Dorling Kindersley:** James Dilley / www.ancientcraft.co.uk. **25 Getty Images:** DEA / Christian Ricci / De Agostini Picture Library (cra). **Klint Janulis:** (crb). **26-27 123RF.com:** Tomasz Trybus / irontrybex. **26 Dorling Kindersley:** James Dilley / www.ancientcraft.co.uk (crb, bl, fbl, br, fbr). **27 Dorling Kindersley:** James Dilley / www.ancientcraft.co.uk (bl, bc, br); Royal Pavilion & Museums, Brighton & Hove (c). **28-29 Dorling Kindersley:** Dan Crisp. **30-31 FLPA:** Tim Fitzharris / Minden Pictures. **31 Getty Images:** John Moore (br). **32 Dorling Kindersley:** James Dilley / www.ancientcraft.co.uk (bl). **33 Dorling Kindersley:** James Dilley / www.ancientcraft.co.uk (t, bl, br). **34 Alamy Stock Photo:** Andrew Walmsley / Alamy Live News (tl). **Klint Janulis:** (bl). **35 Alamy Stock Photo:** Andrew Walmsley (tr). **Dorling Kindersley:** James Dilley / www.ancientcraft.co.uk (tl, br). **Klint Janulis:** (ftr). **36 Alamy Stock Photo:** Michele Burgess (crb). **Dorling Kindersley:** James Dilley / www.ancientcraft.co.uk (bl). **36-37 Alamy Stock Photo:** Paul Williams - FunkyStock / imageBROKER. **37 Alamy Stock Photo:** The Irish Image Collection / Design Pics Inc (clb). **Dorling Kindersley:** James Dilley / www.ancientcraft.co.uk (br). **Getty Images:** Jason Hawkes / Stone (cra). **38-39 Science Photo Library:** Philippe Psaila. **38 Dorling Kindersley:** James Dilley / www.ancientcraft.co.uk (br). **39 Alamy Stock Photo:** Cintract Romain / hemis.fr (cr); Chris Howes / Wild Places Photography (tr). **Dorling Kindersley:** James Dilley / www.ancientcraft.co.uk (clb, crb, br, fbr). **40 Alamy Stock Photo:** Arco Images GmbH / Koehne, K. (bl); World History Archive (c). **40-41 Alamy Stock Photo:** Michiel@BKKPhotography.com. **41 Alamy Stock Photo:** Dinodia Photos RF (t); ImageDB (cra); Steven David Miller / Nature Picture Library (br). **42 Alamy Stock Photo:** The Natural History Museum (crb); Alexey Zarubin (cl); Werner Forman Archive / Heritage Image Partnership Ltd (bc). **Fotolia:** picsfive (clb). **42-43 Alamy Stock Photo:** Lanmas (t). **43 Alamy Stock Photo:** David Wall (bl). **Getty Images:** Homebrew Films Company / Gallo Images (cr). **44 Alamy Stock Photo:** Adrian P. Chinery (bl). **Dorling Kindersley:** Royal Pavilion & Museums, Brighton & Hove (bc). **Dr. Beccy Scott:** (tr). **45 Getty Images:** Dave MacLeod / English Heritage / robertharding (ca). **46 Alamy Stock Photo:** Lanmas (tl). **46-47 Dorling Kindersley:** Dan Crisp. **48-49 Alamy Stock Photo:** Les Gibbon. **49 Dorling Kindersley:** Dan Crisp (tr). **50-51 Getty Images:** Print Collector / Contributor (c/necklace). **50 Dorling Kindersley:** Durham University Oriental Museum (bl); University of Aberdeen (cl); University Museum of Archaeology and Anthropology, Cambridge (bc); Royal Pavilion & Museums, Brighton & Hove (cr). **51 Dorling Kindersley:** James Dilley / www.ancientcraft.co.uk (fbl, bl, cra, cr, crb, br); Royal Pavilion & Museums, Brighton & Hove (c). **Getty Images:** Nathan Benn (tl). **52 Dorling Kindersley:** Royal Pavilion & Museums, Brighton & Hove (fbr); University Museum of Archaeology and Anthropology, Cambridge (bl). **52-53 Dorling Kindersley:** Royal Pavilion & Museums, Brighton & Hove. **53 Alamy Stock Photo:** Diffused Productions (bc); Janzig / Europe (br). **Dorling Kindersley:** Royal Pavilion & Museums, Brighton & Hove (cla, cra, ftr). **54-55 Alamy Stock Photo:** David Lichtneker (t). **55 Alamy Stock Photo:** The Art Archive (bc); Skyscan Photolibrary (tr). **Dorling Kindersley:** Museum of London (br). **56-57 Alamy Stock Photo:** Ariadne Van Zandbergen. **57 Alamy Stock Photo:** Ulrich Doering (tl); PhotoStock-Israel (tr); FLPA (cra); Erez Herrnstadt / Tanzania Africa (cr). **58-59 Alamy Stock Photo:** Incamerastock (b). **South Tyrol Museum Of Archaeology** - www.iceman.it (t). **58 Dorling Kindersley:** Natural History Museum, London (cl); Royal Pavilion & Museums, Brighton & Hove (bl). **59 Alamy Stock Photo:** Granger Historical Picture Archve (br). **Dorling Kindersley:** James Dilley / www.ancientcraft.co.uk (cla). **Dreamstime.com:** Patrick Angevare (cr). **60 Dorling Kindersley:** James Dilley / www.ancientcraft.co.uk (tl, bl). **61 Dorling Kindersley:** James Dilley / www.ancientcraft.co.uk (tl); Royal Pavilion & Museums, Brighton & Hove (br). **64 Dorling Kindersley:** James Dilley / www.ancientcraft.co.uk (tl).

Cover images: Front: Dorling Kindersley: James Dilley / www.ancientcraft.co.uk tr, Royal Pavilion & Museums, Brighton & Hove cra; *Back:* **Dorling Kindersley:** James Dilley / www.ancientcraft.co.uk tr; *Front Flap:* **Dorling Kindersley:** Durham University Oriental Museum tr/ (earrings); **Klint Janulis:** cl; *Back Flap:* **Dorling Kindersley:** Natural History Museum, London crb, University of Aberdeen c; *Front Endpapers:* **Dorling Kindersley:** James Dilley / www.ancientcraft.co.uk (12,000YA sickle), (3.3MYA), (300,000YA); Royal Pavilion & Museums, Brighton & Hove (1.7MYA), (2,000BCE). **Getty Images:** Hulton Fine Art Collection (35,000YA).

All other images © Dorling Kindersley
For further information see: www.dkimages.com

My Findout facts:

Stone Age sites

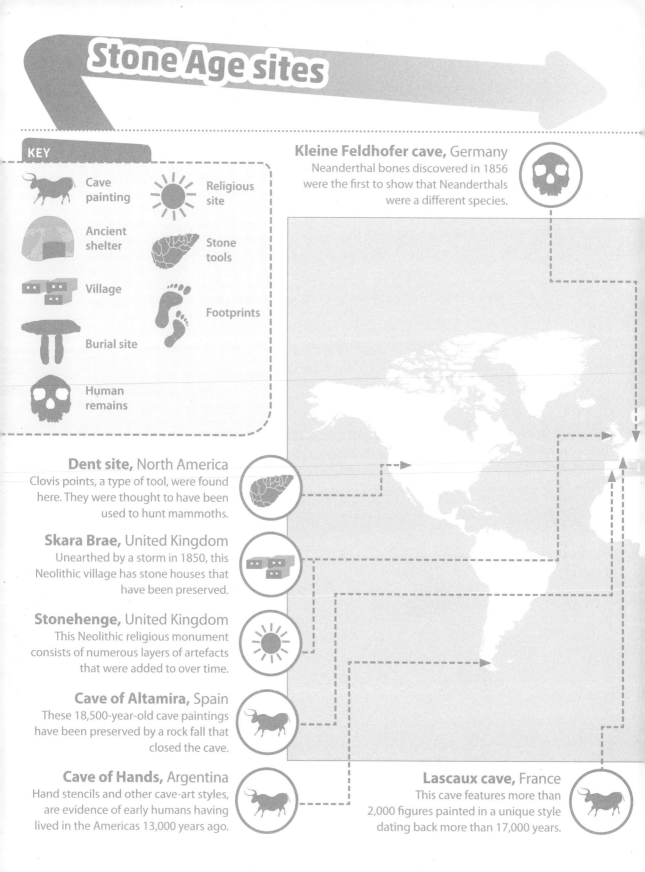

KEY

- Cave painting
- Ancient shelter
- Village
- Burial site
- Human remains
- Religious site
- Stone tools
- Footprints

Kleine Feldhofer cave, Germany
Neanderthal bones discovered in 1856 were the first to show that Neanderthals were a different species.

Dent site, North America
Clovis points, a type of tool, were found here. They were thought to have been used to hunt mammoths.

Skara Brae, United Kingdom
Unearthed by a storm in 1850, this Neolithic village has stone houses that have been preserved.

Stonehenge, United Kingdom
This Neolithic religious monument consists of numerous layers of artefacts that were added to over time.

Cave of Altamira, Spain
These 18,500-year-old cave paintings have been preserved by a rock fall that closed the cave.

Cave of Hands, Argentina
Hand stencils and other cave-art styles, are evidence of early humans having lived in the Americas 13,000 years ago.

Lascaux cave, France
This cave features more than 2,000 figures painted in a unique style dating back more than 17,000 years.

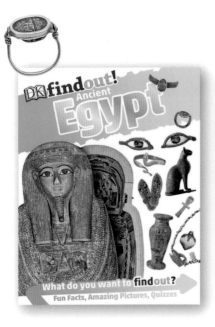

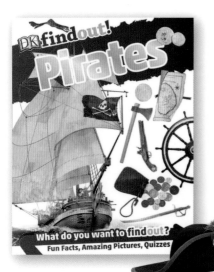

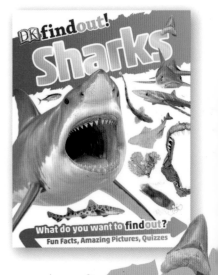

Want to find out more?
Collect them all!

DKfindout! is online!

The only free online encyclopedia a child will ever need!

www.dkfindout.com

Learn about the website

DKfindout!

DKfindout! The free website that brings together brilliant images and key information for children on all the subjects they love.

Up-to-date and verified by experts

"A visual gateway to the world."

Includes videos, galleries, and quizzes!

"Brings learning to life!"

"This is pretty awesome!"

Works on desktop, tablet, and mobile

Visit www.dkfindout.com